THE SINGLE VEGET[ARIAN]

Simple, tasty recipes for one person, using
healthy, natural ingredients

By the same author
THE NATURAL FOODS COOKBOOK
THE WHOLEGRAIN RECIPE BOOK

THE SINGLE VEGETARIAN
Healthy Recipes for One

Marlis Weber

Translated from the German by Linda Sonntag
Illustrated by Juliet Breese

Thorsons
An Imprint of HarperCollinsPublishers

Thorsons
An Imprint of HarperCollins*Publishers*
77–85 Fulham Palace Road,
Hammersmith, London W6 8JB

First published 1985 as Vollwertküche für 1 Person
© Walter Hädecke Verlag, D-7252, Weil der Stadt, Germany
Published by Thorsons 1987
20 19 18 17 16 15 14 13 12 11

© Thorsons Publishing Group 1987

A CIP catalogue record for this book
is available from the British Library

ISBN 0-7225-1358-5

Printed in Great Britain by
Woolnough Bookbinding Limited,
Irthlingborough, Northamptonshire

Contents

Foreword

This book is designed to help all those people living alone to cope with the problems of catering for one.

These problems are not just to do with cooking and eating, they begin when you go out shopping. Most packaged food is designed for more than one person. If you buy a loaf of bread, the chances are that it will be stale before you have got to the last slice. How often have you wished that you could buy just half a loaf of bread or a mini packet of butter?

Then there is the problem of adapting recipes for the single-person household. Most recipes are designed for four people. It would be difficult enough to halve them; quartering them is pretty well impossible.

So single people often feel that it is too much trouble to prepare a meal for themselves. It is easier to grab a bite to eat on the way home from the office, or to live on bread and cheese. Yet the difficulties of catering for one are not insuperable. This book will show that it is possible to enjoy a varied and nourishing diet even if you do live on your own.

It is far simpler to buy convenience foods such as frozen dinners and packet soups of course, but these foods do not have the same nutritional value as natural foods. The long-term consequences of neglecting your body's nutritional needs can be serious. Besides, eating convenience foods gets boring after a while. With a little forethought and a well-planned shopping list, you will find you enjoy preparing and eating nourishing food that is quick, tasty and cheap. Meat and refined foods are expensive, so you will save yourself some money if you cut these out and change to a wholefood diet. Whole grains, milk and dairy products, fresh fruit and

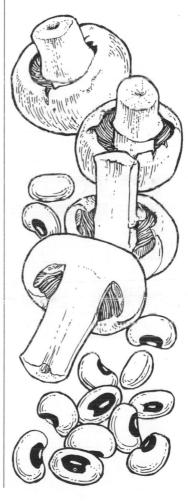

vegetables, nuts and seeds and the oils and fats derived from them will provide you with all the nutrients your body needs, and you can have a healthy diet even if you are on a tight budget.

This book is based on ten years' experience of living alone and catering for one. The aim of the book is to give general information about the value of wholefoods and a healthy diet, as well as providing a complete repertoire of delicious recipes to make healthy eating enjoyable.

Marlis Weber

Introduction

Why is diet important?

Many people do not have a balanced diet. At one end of the scale there is excess. They have too much fat, sugar, salt and alcohol. At the other end of the scale there is a desperate shortage. They do not have enough vitamins, minerals, roughage and liquids

One person in three is overweight and obesity is a common disease. Yet many of us, and this includes children, are suffering from some kind of malnutrition.

The nutritional schizophrenia of the Western world has many differenct causes. Before you can begin to grapple with the problem of your own diet, you need to understand what these causes are.

During the bad times of rationing in the Second World War, when food was scarce and of poor quality, people swore to themselves that when it was over, they would never eat badly again. The result was a frenzy of eating, as soon as more food was available.

This was excusable in the years straight after the war, but soon the excuses began to wear thin. People were simply eating too much.

In the 1950s the diet craze began. The American Gaylord Hauser started a slimming crusade, and his catch-phrase 'The right diet works wonders' swept from Hollywood to Europe. But despite the new fashion, the majority of people carried on eating.

Today you can buy an enormous variety of foods. Massive advertising campaigns present

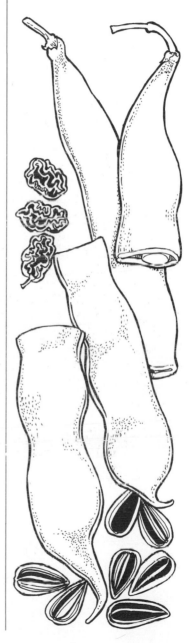

these to us in the most tempting ways, encouraging people to spend more and more on luxury foods.

In our consumer society, people living alone are particularly vulnerable to the temptation of eating for comfort, or to appease loneliness.

These factors show that it is easy enough to become overweight. But how is it that with the huge choice of foodstuffs available, some of us are still undernourished? The reason is that although the variety of foods on sale is wider that ever before, more and more of those foods have been tampered with, added to or refined and rendered worthless.

The refining of foods began in the nineteenth century, when people liked their sugar and their bread to be white. Sugar cane and beet were refined to produce white sugar. The husks were removed from grain to make perfectly white flour. The next step was to refine vegetable oils to make them tasteless, colourless and completely lacking in smell and character.

The demand for convenience foods grew, because these foods need no preparation. They just have to be heated up and they are ready. Packet soups, packet sauces, desserts that are ready in seconds, flour that does not go lumpy, and instant potato all became very popular. Single people especially found these foods ideally suited to their lifestyle. Many households came to rely on them. Their nutritional worth was never questioned.

Today there is a growing concern about convenience foods. They are processed so that they will keep. This processing not only robs them of their nutritional value, but it can also make them harmful because a variety of chemicals are added to them. So, although the calorie content of these foods may be relatively small because of the refining process and the presence of permitted additives.

Convenience foods are quick to prepare and quick to eat because they are bland in taste and texture. But you do not have the same feeling of satisfaction that you do when you eat a proper meal.

The consequences of bad eating habits soon make themselves visible: overweight and an unsightly figure. For many people, the solution is to diet. Fashionable diets are constantly making the headlines and some people crash from one diet to another, subjecting their bodies to all kinds of extremes and doing themselves more harm than good. They may lose weight in the short term, but constant dieting does long-term damage and pangs of guilt are just as painful as pangs of hunger.

The real solution is to take a new look at your eating habits, and to give up faddy or punishingly strict diets in favour of a healthy eating plan that you can stick to permanently. Wholefoods do not take a long time to prepare, they are not expensive or difficult to use and they are not tasteless. They are delicious. And creating a healthy meal that tastes good is an enjoyable pursuit, not a chore.

If you have had a long period of unhealthy eating, you can take some sensible steps to put things right.

For example, if you have nothing but whey or juice for a while this will rid your body of harmful substances. There is more about this aspect at the end of the book.

As a single person changing to wholefood eating, you have an enormous advantage, you have no one to please but yourself. If you had a family to cater for, and not everyone was interested in healthy eating, it would be more difficult to make the change. And once you have become a competent wholefood cook, you can invite your friends to sample your new way of eating.

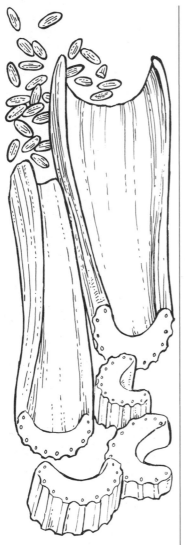

What is a Wholefood Diet?

A healthy body needs certain essential elements such as amino acids, fatty acids, minerals, vitamins, carbohydrates and sufficient water. These are all contained in a wholefood diet.

Other substances, such as chemicals, harm the body. Foods containing harmful additives should be kept to a minimum or preferably cut out altogether.

When planning a healthy balanced diet, the following points are worth remembering.

- Your food intake should correspond to your energy requirements. Keep a set of scales in the bathroom and check your weight.
- Your diet should contain natural foods, with as few refined or processed foods as possible. It should include wholegrains and wholemeal products, milk and dairy products, fresh fruit and vegetables, nuts and seeds and the oils pressed from them.
- Eat only top quality foodstuffs, preferably those which have been organically grown. Where possible, avoid foods that contain additives, colourings, flavourings and preservatives. Only buy clean, undamaged goods.
- Everything you eat should be wholesome.
- Food should not be too fatty, too sweet or too salty.
- Eat only the things you enjoy eating.

A Few Rules for Wholefood Eating

You cannot enjoy your food if you gulp it down.

Try to eat slowly, so that you can really taste it. When you get up in the morning have a good breakfast and make sure you chew each mouthful, rather than munching a piece of toast as you race out of the house.

When you wake up drink a cup of your favourite herbal tea with a spoonful of honey or a squeeze of lemon juice.

Try eating wholegrains at breakfast time. Tempt yourself with the suggestions on page 28. Wholemeal cereals will satisfy you and stave off lunchtime hunger for longer. They keep better than other cereals too.

If you have not already done so, introduce quark into your diet. Eat it as a savoury, with herbs, sprouts and chopped vegetables, or as a sweet, with fresh and dried fruit and nuts and a little honey.

Always begin your main meals with raw vegetables dressed with cold-pressed oils. Raw vegetables are more nutritious than cooked ones. They are also more satisfying, so that you need less of them.

Avoid fatty foods, especially fatty meat and sausages. There are plenty of alternatives to these cholesterol-rich foods, which may also contain hormones and other additives.

Spread butter and margarine thinly on your bread. Do without it when you can. Alternate between butter and polyunsaturated margarine.

Cut out sugar completely. Sugar adds unnecessary calories and does not satisfy hunger. Sweeten food with a little honey, maple syrup, fructose, fresh or dried fruit, or fruit juice concentrate.

Be sparing in your use of salt. Use more herbs and spices instead.

Cut out white flour altogether and use wholemeal flour. Avoid anything made from white flour, such as pasta. Use wholewheat pasta instead.

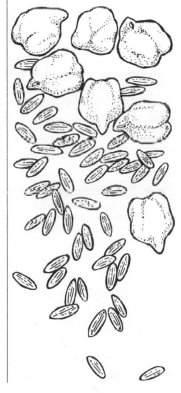

Wholefood is more bulky and satisfying than processed food. It is also more tasty and chewy, so you do not need to add so many flavourings such as salt and sweeteners.

Drink milk and unsweetened fruit and vegetable juice (but watch the calories!), mineral water and herbal teas. Add a little fruit juice to herbal tea for a change, or add a slice of orange, lemon or apple.

If you want a snack to munch while you are travelling or out on a walk, take some wholemeal biscuits or dried fruit with you.

Make sure you store foods correctly so that they do not lose their nutritional value. Prepare them correctly, too (see page 42).

When you are cooking, use only the best butter and oils and the freshest herbs. Single people may be tempted to eat food that is past its best rather than waste it, but it is important to use fresh food in perfect condition and cook it as simply as possible.

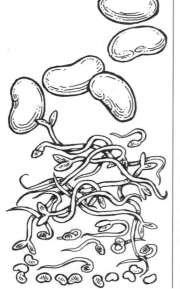

An A to Z of Wholefoods and Diet Facts

Agar-agar is derived from seaweed and has a high mineral content. In vegetarian cooking it is used as a thickening agent for sauces, and as a gelling agent instead of gelatine.

Alfalfa are the seeds of the lucerne plant. Like grains and pulses, these seeds are very good for sprouting.

Coconut fat is soft vegetable fat which is suitable for frying. It is low in polyunsaturates.

Eggs are a natural food and have an important place in the wholefood diet. They should be eaten in moderation because of their high cholesterol content. They also contain 10 per cent fat. Free-range eggs are best.

Enzymes are substances found in all living organisms and their presence signifies that a foodstuff is 'alive'. They are killed at a temperature of 50°C.

Fatty acids are foundation stones of fats, and they have different saturation levels. Polyunsaturated fats are an essential part of the healthy diet.

Fibre is the name given to indigestible substances which swell in the bowel, thus stimulating it into activity. Principle sources of fibre or roughage are wholegrains, nuts, seeds, vegetables (roots and tubers) and fruit. Our intake of fibre is often insufficient.

Honey is a natural sweetener with many valuable qualities besides its high sugar content.

Linseed has a high fibre content. It swells well and lubricates the bowel, and is therefore prescribed for stomach and bowel upsets. Take it crushed for stomach ulcers and whole for constipation.

Malnutrition is a condition caused by starvation or, in the Western world, by an unbalanced diet which is lacking in vital nutrients.

Maple syrup is made from the concentrated sap of the maple tree and comes from Canada. It contains minerals and trace elements. Its very individual taste goes especially well with pancakes, waffles and muesli.

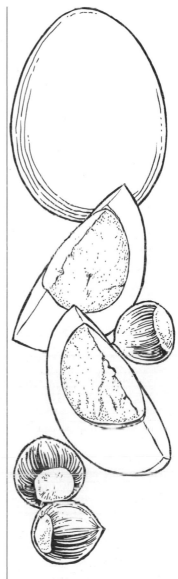

Nut pulp is made entirely without additives. It is suitable for spreading on bread, for baking and for making sauces and desserts.

Pear juice or apple juice concentrate can be used as an alternative to sugar. It can also be spread on bread.

Residue is the name for substances such as hormones and chemical feeds used in the rearing of animals, and chemical weedkillers and fertilizers in the cultivation of crops, that are still present in the food to some degree when it reaches the table.

Sea salt contains sodium and other minerals, such as iodine, magnesium and calcium. Do not use too much salt.

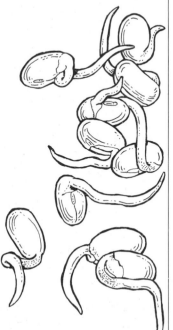

Soya beans are rich in protein and they are also highly versatile. Soya bean sprouts are a valuable raw food. Soya flour can be used in baking and to thicken soups and sauces. Because of its high lecithin content it can be used to a certain extent as an egg substitute. Soya milk is a valuable alternative to cow's milk for those who are allergic to it. Tofu, which is similar to quark, is made from soya milk with the help of a coagulate. Soya sauce is made by the fermentation of the soya bean. Soya products, both dried and conserved, are available in many different flavours as an alternative to meat. Because the soya bean is so nutritious and useful it is becoming more and more important as a food all over the world.

Tofu see soya beans.

Whey is the part of the milk left behind when the curds are separated out to make cheese. It is rich in protein, vitamins and minerals.

Wholemeal breadcrumbs can be made from wholemeal bread in the food processor. You can also buy ready-made breadcrumbs.

Yeast for bread-making can be bought dried or fresh or made at home. Mix 3 dessertspoons of crushed rye with a little lukewarm water and some honey and leave it to stand for a few days, stirring from time to time.

Yeast products are a source of protein and B-group vitamins. Use salted or unsalted yeast extract as a spread for bread or a seasoning for hotpots. Or dissolve it in hot water for a nourishing drink, which can also be used as the basis for a vegetable soup.

Using Herbs

If you use a lot of fresh herbs it is best to grow them yourself. Most herbs are quite undemanding and will survive equally well in the garden, in a window box or in a pot on the window sill. They need a light, sunny position, good soil enriched with a natural fertilizer, fresh air and regular watering with clean fresh water. Watering is especially important if they are in a pot or tub.

Growing your own herbs is particularly useful if you are living alone, because you can snip off a few leaves as you need them. If you buy fresh herbs, some may be wasted because you cannot use them quickly enough. If you cannot grow your own, however, you should buy them in the smallest possible quantities and keep them well wrapped in the fridge. In times of plenty you can lay in a store for the winter, when fresh herbs are difficult to come by. Sprigs of parsley, dill, chervil and others can be snipped into useful

portions and frozen in ice cube trays or other small plastic containers.

You can also use dried herbs. Herbs such as thyme and sage are better suited to drying. After you have harvested the plants, break them up into single springs or tie them together loosely in bunches. Make sure that air can get between the stems or they will go mouldy before they dry. When they have dried, pull off the leaves or flowers and store them in dark glass jars with airtight screw tops.

Herbs should be prepared carefully so that they do not lose their flavour. Never let them stand in water. Just give them a quick rinse in cold water, then shake them and pat them dry on absorbent kitchen paper.

Chop them on a clean board with a very sharp kitchen knife or, ideally, with a two-handled knife that you can rock back and forth over them. It is easier to cut some herbs, such as dill and chives with a sharp pair of scissors.

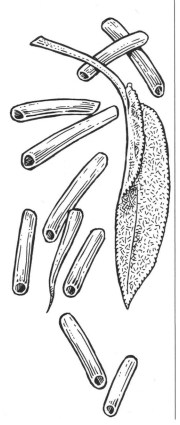

Rub dried herbs between first finger and thumb as you drop them into the cooking pot. This releases their aroma. A pestle and mortar are useful additions to your kitchen equipment. You can use them to grind spices such as coriander, fennel and anis.

Herbs are not only used to flavour food. They also have a direct influence on the appetite and the digestion because they contain vitamins and minerals. This is why many herbs and aromatic plants, when taken regularly and in sufficient quantities, can ward off certain illnesses. For example, garlic has a beneficial effect on the blood vessels, and parsley and nettles on the kidneys.

Another advantage of using herbs and spices for flavouring is that you will need less salt. It is now known that many people consume far too much salt, and that salt can be responsible for high blood-pressure.

The following herbs are useful ones to grow or keep in the store cupboard.

Basil. The taste of basil is both sweet and strong. It can be used fresh or dried, but only use a little at a time. Basil is good in salads, vegetable dishes, sauces and anything containing tomatoes. Add it to a herb dressing, either on its own or mixed with other herbs.

Borage. The smell of borage is strongly reminiscent of freshly cut cucumber. It makes a good salad herb and is particularly delicious on cucumber salad.

Dill is fine-leaved and feathery, and has a pleasantly sweet smell. Fresh dill has far more flavour than the dried variety. It goes well with many types of salad and tastes good mixed with butter or quark and spread on fresh bread or potatoes.

Tarragon has a mild yet distinctive taste. Fresh tarragon is best, though you can buy it dried. Tarragon vinegar is very popular, and you can make this at home, it makes a welcome gift for lovers of wholefood cooking.

Chervil has an aromatic smell and sweet taste. Dried chervil has hardly any taste, so it is only worth using this herb fresh. It goes with salads, in spreads and on vegetable dishes.

Garlic has a very individual and pungent smell and a taste that is both sweet and sharp. Use whole garlic cloves or dried garlic powder. Only the smallest amount of garlic is needed to flavour a dish. Often just rubbing a salad bowl with a cut clove of garlic is enough.

Watercress. The leaves and stalks of the plant

have a sharp peppery taste reminiscent of radish. Watercress is rich in vitamins and minerals and should always be used fresh.

Horseradish has a burning sharp taste and can only be used grated. Grated horseradish goes brown in the air and should be put in milk or lemon juice to stop this happening. It tastes good with beetroot.

Marjoram has a strong aromatic smell and a spicy, slightly bitter taste. Sprinkle the fresh leaves on bread and butter or on a tomato salad. Dried marjoram is widely available and it keeps its aroma well.

Parsley. The curly-leaved variety is most common, but there is also a flat-leaved, slightly more aromatic type. Parsley should be eaten fresh so that it retains its high vitamin C content. It makes a valuable addition to salads and vegetable dishes, and goes very well with dill, chervil, chives and balm.

Pepper. Black peppercorns are the green, unripe berries of the plant which are fermented. White pepper comes from the ripened berries. The hard corns can be ground in a pepper mill at home, or you can buy ground pepper. Ground pepper has a very strong, hot flavour and makes fatty foods more easily digestible. Almost all savoury foods can be seasoned with ground pepper.

Burnet has a cucumber-like taste, well suited to young green salad vegetables, tomato salads and sauces.

Sorrel contains large quantities of vitamin C and iron and purifies the blood. It tastes good in green salads, with quark and in sauces.

Thyme has a strong smell and taste. For this reason it should always be used sparingly. Thyme comes second only to marjoram for popularity amongst French and Italian cooks.

Vanilla has a mild, delicate and very pleasant flavour and is deservedly popular. It can be bought in the form of beans or pods or liquid vanilla flavouring. The fruit are fermented in a moist environment before they are fully ripe. During this process they turn dark brown in colour and develop their full aroma. Vanilla can be used to flavour milk desserts, cream, ices, chocolate and fruit. It is also often used in baking.

Lemon balm has a fresh spicy taste, very reminiscent of lemon. The leaves are at their most aromatic when freshly picked. They taste good in green salads and fruit salads, and also go well in drinks.

Using the recipes

All the recipes in this book have been tried and tested several times. I hope that they will work at the first attempt, even for inexperienced cooks. If a recipe does go wrong, don't give up. Try it again, perhaps giving yourself more preparation time.

When I put the menus together I was careful to make sure that all the ingredients of each course complemented each other. The menus are designed to be satisfying and should not take too much time or energy to prepare. However, they are only suggestions. If the menus seem too extensive, you can follow the suggestions given in the recipes for dishes to accompany them.

Some dishes can be reheated without losing

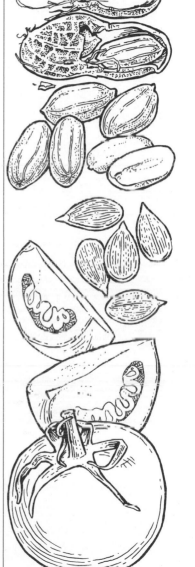

taste, and quality so I have suggested that you make two portions, one for now and one for later.

If a recipe does not use up all the ingredients you have bought, you can follow the suggestions for using leftovers.

If you keep to the recommended cooking times, you will not lose any of the nutritional value of the food. Make sure that you store and prepare food correctly so that you avoid the build-up of toxic substances, such as the highly poisonous toxins that develop in mould growing on bread and nuts.

Keep a store of the ingredients you find yourself using over and over again in the recipes. You can store the following foods in screw-topped jars in the refrigerator:

- Salad dressings (without herbs) for a few days.
- Quark toppings for up to two days.
- Grated cheese for several days.
- Wholemeal breadcrumbs for a couple of weeks.
- Chopped nuts for a few days.

Always make sure that the screw top is tightly closed.

Good quality lemon juice is available in bottles. Often it is not worth cutting into a whole fruit for one person.

Make your own seasoned oil. Pour good quality vegetable oil into small dark glass jars and add different herbs and seasonings. After a few weeks it will taste excellent. Fresh soft white cheese, goat's cheese and sheep's cheese can be stored in flavoured oil for up to three weeks. Try this with tofu too.

Buy a few small airtight plastic containers to store food in the fridge. This way you will save on foil and cling wrap.

Gadgets and equipment you will need

If you search through your kitchen cupboards, you will probably be surprised to find how much equipment you have accumulated. Doubtless some of it is very useful, but some of it you will hardly ever use, and there may be things you hardly even recognize.

Don't let yourself be blinded by slick advertising. Consider carefully whether you will really use something before you buy it.

In a one-person household you can get away with relatively few gadgets. If you are setting up your kitchen for the first time, then it is a good idea to buy the most expensive things you can afford, even if you have to buy them gradually. This way, the equipment you buy will last.

The following suggestions do not cover kitchen furniture or china. They are merely a guide to some of the most important items in the single person's kitchen.

Fridge/freezer. Most people have a fridge nowadays. Where possibe, choose a fridge with a three star freezing compartment. If you can afford it, buy a small freezer. A lot of recipes can be made in larger quantities, divided into individual portions and frozen, without loss of nutritive value. Bread, bread rolls, cakes, butter, margarine and cheese can all be stored frozen.

Table grill. A small electric table grill is a practical gadget, as it uses less electricity than the grill on an electric oven, and can also be used for toasting.

Pots and pans. You will need a heavy-based frying pan made of stainless steel or cast iron and of a decent size (about 30cm/12 inches in diameter). Good quality saucepans are essential. To start with, you will want one that holds 3 – 4 litres, a fairly tall 2-litre capacity pan and a shallow 1 litre pan. It is never worth buying cheap pots and pans.

Kitchen utensils. Every kitchen needs a selection of spatulas, ladles and slotted spoons, and a pair of kitchen scissors. These are basic necessities and you should buy the best quality you can afford.

A can opener is an essential item in any kitchen. People with weak wrists will also find a twist-off opener for screw tops very useful.

Choose a small whisk, suitable for whisking small amounts of egg white and so on. A large whisk will keep tipping up and falling out of a small bowl. Choose a good quality whisk that is not too light.

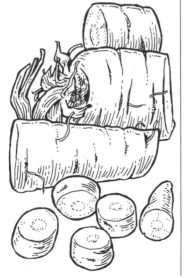

Knives are always a problem because good knives are very expensive, but cheap ones are useless. The solution might to be replace your cheap knives with good ones as you can afford them. It is a good idea to have two small vegetable knives (one with a curved blade and the other with a straight blade) a large heavy chef's knife with a broad straight blade, and a large knife with a serrated blade for cutting tomatoes. You will also need a peeler for vegetables like potatoes and asparagus.

Another essential is a good wooden chopping board.

Grater. Raw vegetables can be grated in a food processor if you can afford one, but a hand-held grater is all you really need for this task. It should have blades with various sized holes. Use it for grating cheese too.

Electric mixer. This is a very useful gadget, even in the single person kitchen.

Tins and moulds. Buy a selection of useful sized tins and moulds for cakes and pies. Remember that a large pie will probably be past its best before you get to the end of it, so small pie tins will be more useful.

Mortars and mills. A mortar is a very useful piece of kitchen equipment. Whole herbs and spices can be pounded to release their full aroma. Two or three ingredients can be pounded together so that the flavours merge completely. The best sort of mortars are made of glass or marble.

Spice mills can be bought gradually. Begin with a pepper mill. You will find a mill very useful for cumin and coriander and other spices used in bread making. It is better to buy whole spices and grind them yourself, especially in a one-person household, because they keep for longer.

You can also invest in a grain mill to make your own flour. These can be bought in specialist cookery equipment shops.

Garlic lovers will want a garlic press. Make sure that the one you buy has a small plate in front of the holes to stop them getting clogged.

Mini-graters are available for nutmeg, horseradish and lemon zest.

Sieves. You need a large sieve for making soups and a smaller sieve or tea strainer. Make sure they are made of stainless steel. A plastic colander with large holes is useful for draining fruit and vegetables.

Ovenproof dishes. You will need a selection of small ovenproof dishes made of pyrex or cast iron.

Of course there are plenty of other useful gadgets, such as funnels, measuring jugs, tongs, citrus squeezers, egg slicers, syringes, spatter guards to put on top of frying pans, pins for puncturing egg shells, and so on.

But it is best to decide what else you need as you go along. This saves buying equipment you may never use.

Breakfasts and Elevenses

Are you a person who grabs a quick breakfast as you rush off to work? Perhaps you miss breakfast altogether. If so you are depriving yourself of the most important meal of the day.

Every day should begin peacefully with a wholesome breakfast. There is no better time to enjoy wholemeal foods, such as porridge, pancakes, bread, waffles or muesli This chapter contains lots of ideas to choose from. Experiment with them all and then stick to your favourites.

Sometimes you will need to plan ahead. The meal may need to be prepared and soaked the night before to make it easily digestible.

If you are new to wholefoods, it is probably a good idea to start off with muesli. The great Swiss doctor Bircher-Benner prescribed it for his patients, and today it is one of Switzerland's national dishes.

Dr Bircher-Benner's Original Muesli Recipe

(Must be prepared the evening before.)

Mix the oats with a little water and leave to soften for a while. Stir in the cream and lemon juice. You can also add a little honey to taste. Wash the apple well and grate it with its peel. Mix the apple and nuts into the muesli.

250 kcal   1000 kJ

1-2 dessertspoons wholemeal oat flakes
A little water
2-3 dessertspoons fresh cream
1 teaspoon lemon juice
1 medium apple
1 dessertspoon chopped nuts

Cracked Wheat Muesli

280 kcal   1120 kJ

(Must be prepared the evening before.)

2 dessertspoons cracked wheat (the coarse variety), softened overnight in a little water
1 small carton live yogurt
1 medium apple
1 teaspoon honey
1 dessertspoon coarsely chopped nuts

Mix the softened cracked wheat with the yogurt. Wash the apple well and grate it into the muesli. Add honey and sprinkle with chopped nuts.

Muesli with Germinated Corn

300 kcal   1200 kJ

2 dessertspoons germinated corn (see page 52)
1 small carton (150g) soured cream, or buttermilk
1 banana
Juice of half a lemon (store the other half in the fridge)
1 dessertspoon currants

Stir together the corn and soured cream or buttermilk. Mash in the banana with a fork to release its full flavour, add the lemon juice and currants and mix well.

Carrot Muesli with Bran

200 kcal   800 kJ

2 medium carrots
Juice of 1 orange
1 teaspoon honey
2 dessertspoons bran
1 dessertspoon sunflower seeds

Peel the carrots if necessary, then grate them finely. Mix with the orange juice and honey. Stir in the bran and sprinkle with sunflower seeds.

Muesli with Berries and Cream

Soften the oats in the orange juice. Wash the berries, remove the stalks and add them to the oats with the maple syrup. Mix well and top with the cream, which may be whipped first.

280 kcal   1120 kJ

1-2 dessertspoons oat flakes
2-3 dessertspoons orange juice
6oz (150g) ripe berries of your choice
1 teaspoon maple syrup
5 dessertspoons fresh cream

Millet Flake Muesli

Put the buttermilk in a dish and mix in the sesame seeds, the mashed banana or the finely grated apple. Stir in the honey. Mix in the millet flakes just before you eat the muesli (they soften very quickly).

200 kcal   800 kJ

1 glass buttermilk
1 teaspoon sesame seeds
1 banana or 1 apple
1 teaspoon honey
2 dessert spoons millet flakes

Grits with Honey

Pour the barley grits (which can be softened beforehand if there is time) into boiling water, add the salt and lemon peel and cook over a gentle heat for about 10 minutes until the grits are well swollen. Meanwhile, heat the butter in a pan and brown the almonds in it. Let the nuts cool, then stir them into the grits with the honey. Top with cream. This dish also tastes good with cinnamon instead of the almonds.

*Pare the lemon rind very finely so that the fruit will keep.

350 kcal   1400 kJ

3-4 dessertspoons medium barley grits
7-8 fl oz (200-250ml) water
Sea salt
A little lemon peel*
⅓oz (10g) butter
1 dessertspoon chopped almonds
1 dessertspoon honey
2-3 dessertspoons fresh cream

250 kcal   1000 kJ

7-8 fl oz (200-250 ml)
water
3-4 dessertspoons coarse
oat flakes
Sea salt
1 dessertspoon currants
Cold milk or cream

Porridge with Currants

Bring the water to the boil. Pour on the oats and cook over a gentle heat for about 15 minutes, until well swollen. Add salt and the currants and continue cooking until the currants are plump. Pour the porridge into a deep plate and eat with cold milk or cream.

300 kcal   1200 kJ

2 dessertspoons mixed
crushed wholegrains
A little water
1 glass full cream milk
5oz (125g) berries of
your choice
Anis
Coriander
1 teaspoon honey or
maple syrup

Wholemeal Porridge with Full Cream Milk

Pour water over the grain and allow to soften overnight in the fridge. Stir in the full cream milk. Add the berries and a little crushed anis and coriander, then stir in honey to taste.

A few alternatives

There are lots of other good things for breakfast too.

Wholemeal bread and bread rolls can be spread with low fat cheese or quark, flavoured with fruit or herbs, or with homemade spreads or honey.

If there is time, treat yourself to a pancake with maple syrup.

Drink freshly pressed juice to refresh you and herbal tea to stimulate the metabolism.

Cereals — which to choose

Whole cereal grain must be treated or prepared
in one way or another before its nutrients can be
properly ingested into the body. There are several
ways in which this can be done:

Germination. Wholegrains are at their most
nutritious when they are freshly germinated (see
page 52).

Cracked and softened. When cracked grains are
soaked in a very little water (they will taste
watery if you use too much), they soften and
swell. Their nutritive value is increased and they
become easily digestible. Grains can be softened
in the refrigerator overnight.

Cooking. Cooking makes cereals more digestible,
but it does detract slightly from their nutritive
value. Heat always has a detrimental effect on
vitamins and enzymes.

Drying. Wholegrains can be dried at a
temperature of 70°C in the oven. The grains
open up and become more digestible, but retain
more of their nutritive value than when boiled.
  Many cereals are available in the form of
flakes, but when you buy them you should make
sure that they are wholemeal flakes, that is to
say that the germ of the grain (as in the
wheatgerm) is still present. Flakes are
commercially produced by causing the grain to
swell in warm damp conditions and then
crushing it flat. Cereal flakes do not have the full
nutritive value of raw wholegrains, but many
people find them more easily digestible.

Alternative spreads for bread

Spreads for bread often seem to be sadly lacking in variety. Paté is unacceptable for the wholefood lover, but the vegetarian alternatives can be very uninspiring and always choosing cheese is boring indeed. Why not make your own spreads for supper or a snack? They are easily stored in the fridge.

The following recipe for savoury butter (you can use soft vegetable margarine instead) can be prepared well in advance, wrapped in foil and stored in the freezer. If unexpected guests arrive, simply defrost the butter and serve it with jacket potatoes and a raw salad.

Savoury Butter

**5-8oz (125-250g) butter
A little sea salt
Freshly ground black pepper**
   with crushed garlic
   or **chopped herbs**
   or **yeast extract (tastes especially good)**
   or **tomato purée**
   or **sage leaves**
   or **lightly toasted sesame seeds**

The butter should be soft and creamy (beat it with an electric beater if possible) before you add the flavouring of your choice. You can prepare this in advance and freeze it.

Camembert Cream with Onions

220 kcal 880 kJ

Pound the Camembert to a cream or cut it up finely. Chop the onion finely and mix it with the cheese, paprika and chives. Sprinkle on the sunflower seeds. Tastes especially good on wholemeal bread.

½ portion camembert cheese (45 per cent fat, very ripe)
1 small onion
Paprika pepper
1 dessertspoon chopped chives
1 teaspoon sunflower seeds

Pears with Roquefort Cream

240 kcal 960 kJ

Put the cheese in a plastic container and immerse it briefly in hot water. Pound it to a cream with the quark. Wash the pear and cut it into eight pieces. Remove the stalk and the core. Spread the cream cheese on wholemeal toast and lay the pear on top.

2oz (50g) Roquefort or Gorgonzola cheese (50 per cent fat)
2 dessertspoons quark (20 per cent fat)
1 ripe pear
1 teaspoon lemon juice

Aubergine Pâté

180 kcal 720 kJ

Remove the skin from the cooked aubergine and purée the flesh. Peel and chop the onion and cook it in oil until soft and transparent. Add the aubergine purée and the tomato paste and cook gently for a few minutes to let the flavours mingle. Season with salt, pepper, coriander and parsley. A delicious topping for wholemeal toast.

1 small aubergine (or half from the day before), sliced and cooked in oil
1 small onion
A little olive oil or walnut oil
1 teaspoon tomato purée
Sea salt
White pepper
Crushed coriander to taste
1 dessertspoon chopped flat-leaved parsley

170 kcal   680 kJ

½ carton soured cream
(use the rest on muesli
or jacket potatoes)
1 dessertspoon quark
(use the rest for dessert
the next day)
1 teaspoon horseradish,
freshly grated or from a
jar
1 small apple
Sea salt (optional)

Horseradish and Apple Spread

Combine all the ingredients well and season with
sea salt if liked.

1 dessertspoon =
100 kcal   400 kJ

About 2oz (50g)
hazelnuts
5-7 walnuts
1 dessertspoon sesame
seeds
4oz (100g) butter
1 dessertspoon honey

Homemade Nut Cream

(This spread keeps for 2-3 weeks in the fridge.)

Put the hazelnuts with the walnuts, which you
have chopped coarsely, in a pan and toast them
lightly. Crush them together. Toast the sesame
seeds. Cream the butter (beat it with an electric
beater for preference) and mix in the nuts and
honey.

Packed Snacks

Hunger pangs can be avoided by eating little and
often rather than having very large meals. Small
snacks in between meals are a good idea
whether you are at home or at work. Plan them
so that they are nourishng and can be packed
for travelling. If you take a snack to work it
should look as appetising when you unpack it as
when you prepared it.

Interesting Cheese Sandwiches

Spread wholemeal bread or rolls thinly with butter. Fill with lettuce, cucumber and sliced cheese.	180 kcal 720 kJ
Spread wholemeal bread or rolls thinly with butter, then with yeast extract or tomato purée. Fill with sliced Camembert.	190 kcal 760 kJ
Spread wholemeal bread or rolls thinly with low fat white cheese and fill with apple slices. (Any leftovers can be eaten with muesli.)	190 kcal 760 kJ

Inspired Vegetarian Pâté Sandwiches

160 kcal 640 kJ

Spread wholemeal bread with vegetarian pâté and fill with slices of olive, tomato and strips of red, green or yellow pepper

Crispbread with Bananas and Nuts

170 kcal 640 kJ

Spread 2 crispbreads with butter, top with banana slices and sprinkle with chopped nuts.

Packet muesli makes a good in-between-times snack that you can keep in your office drawer. Eat it with buttermilk or full cream milk and perhaps raw carrot sticks, slices of cucumber, radishes, strips of red or green pepper, apples, pears, dried fruit or chopped nuts. There are more suggestions throughout the book for meals that you can take to work.

Oven-Toasted Treats

Toasted treats taste much better with wholemeal bread.

Baked Asparagus on Toast

300 kcal   1200 kJ

Toast the bread lightly and sprinkle with grated cheese. Peel the asparagus spears well and cook in lightly salted water for about 10 minutes. Cut each spear in half and lay on top of the cheese. Sprinkle with paprika and top with the remaining cheese. Bake in a preheated oven at 200°C (400°F, Gas Mark 6) for about 15 minutes. Garnish with slices of tomato. Tastes good with spinach salad.

2 slices wholemeal bread
2 dessertspoons grated cheese (45 per cent fat)
6-8 asparagus spears
Paprika pepper
1 tomato

Toast with Fresh White Cheese and Basil

250 kcal   1000 kJ

Toast the bread briefly and spread with margarine. Slice the tomato, lay on the bread and season lightly. Crumble the cheese on top and bake for about 15 minutes in a preheated oven at 200°C (400°F, Gas Mark 6). Garnish with fresh basil. Tastes good with a crisp salad of Iceberg lettuce.

2 slices wholemeal bread
⅓oz (10g) soft vegetable margarine
2 medium tomatoes
Celery salt
2oz (50g) fresh white cheese (fromage frais)
Fresh basil leaves

320 kcal   1280 kJ

2 slices wholemeal
bread
1 portion Camembert
cheese (45 per cent fat)
2 teaspoons cranberries
(from a jar)
1 pinch powdered cloves
1 teaspoon butter
2 dessertspoons
chopped parsley

Toast with Camembert and Cranberries

Toast the bread lightly, then top with slices of Camembert. Make a dent in the middle of each and add 1 teaspoon cranberries. Season with cloves and top with small flakes of butter. Bake in a preheated oven at 200°C (400°F, Gas Mark 6) for about 15 minutes, then sprinkle with parsley. Tastes good with raw kohlrabi salad.

320 kcal   1280 kJ

2 slices wholemeal
bread
⅓oz (10g) soft vegetable
margarine
1 teaspoon freshly
grated horseradish
1 ripe peach
Celery salt
2 slices Edam cheese (45
per cent fat)

Toast with Peach and Horseradish

Toast the bread lightly, then spread with the margarine mixed with the horseradish. Immerse the peach briefly in boiling water and remove the skin. Cut it into slices and lay them on the toast, season lightly with celery salt and cover with cheese. Bake in a preheated oven at 200°C (400°F, Gas Mark 6) for 15-20 minutes. Tastes good with a raw celery salad.

Raw Vegetables and Salads

Vegetables, like fruit, are rich in essential nutrients, such as vitamins, minerals and fibre, but the effectiveness of these substances is greatly reduced by cooking. It is far better to eat them raw whenever possible.

Raw vegetables should be eaten at every meal. Because they are so easy to prepare, they are a practical addition to the diet of every single person, as well as being very healthy.

And you can be sure that raw vegetables will always go with whatever else you are planning to eat. Eat them to begin a meal instead of soup, as an accompaniment, is a main dish on a hot summer's day, as a snack, or as a slimmer's evening meal.

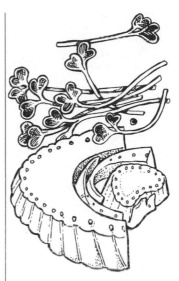

Oils for dressings

Good quality vegetable oils play an important role in wholefood cooking. They are particularly valuable in the preparation of raw vegetable dishes and salads. Always choose cold-pressed unrefined oils which are high in polyunsaturates and also contain vitamin E, lecithin and their original colour and flavour. Unrefined oils have their own individual taste which will bring out the flavours in your salad.

Handle these natural products with care. Keep oil tightly sealed in a cool dark place and use it within about twelve weeks of opening the bottle (linseed oil should be used within two weeks). The single person will be better off buying small bottles of oil even if they seem more expensive.

Though these oils are normally used cold,

they can also be used for frying and sometimes for a very short cooking period in the oven. They should not be used for frying at very high temperatures.

The following are all recommended oils, but every reader will find his own personal favourite, which may be used as a substitute for any of the others:

Linseed oil comes from the seeds of flax, from which linen is made. It has a high content of essential fatty acids. Cold-pressed linseed oil has an unusual flavour. It must be used within two weeks of opening the bottle because it is sensitive to oxygen.

Olive oil is derived from the fruit of the olive tree. The best quality olive oil is the so-called virgin or extra virgin oil, which is the oil from the first pressing. Olive oil has a strongly individual flavour and is particularly good for the digestion.

Sunflower oil is derived from selected sunflower seeds. It is an essential ingredient in the kitchen of any wholefood cook because of its unobtrusive flavour, and it is also recommended for its high fatty acid and vitamin E content.

Oil of wheatgerm is expensive because a large amount of wheat is needed to produce a small quantity of oil. It has a very high vitamin E content and a pleasantly wheaty taste and it is extremely nutritious.

Walnut oil is derived from the ripe fruit of the walnut tree. It has a fine nutty aroma and is delicious as a dressing on delicate salads.

Tips for preparing raw vegetables and salads

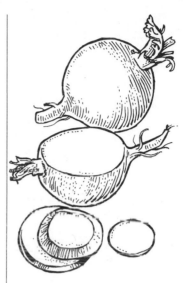

It is difficult to give exact quantities in recipes for raw vegetables, and also to specify exactly how much dressing you will need, as it depends so much on personal preference.

You might like your salad quite smooth and oily, or you might prefer it without any dressing at all. Some like dressings with vinegar or lemon juice and herbs, many people like garlic and onions, and others prefer honey and vanilla in their salads. It really is up to the individual. This is why alternative dressings are given in the following recipes.

With each of the salad recipes I have suggested a dressing which goes particularly well with that dish. However, there are so many to choose from that you can change them around when you have discovered which ones you like best.

Cleaning
All vegetables should be rinsed very thoroughly. Take special care with anything with curly leaves or a hairy skin, both of which may harbour dirt.

Water-soluble substances such as vitamin C, vitamins of the B group and minerals can be lost if they come into direct contact with water. Therefore all vegetables, herbs and fruit should be washed whole. Never cut into a vegetable before you wash it.

Preparing and cutting
Substances sensitive to oxygen, such as vitamins A and C, will be lost if fruit and vegetables are cut and left before being eaten. For this reason, you should prepare them at the last possible minute. If you have to prepare them in advance,

cover them tightly with cling film and leave them in a cool dark place until you are ready to eat.

Important notes:
- Where possible, buy organically-grown fruit and vegetables.
- Only use the freshest ingredients.
- Wash fruit and vegetables quickly but thoroughly.
- Do not cut fruit and vegetables before washing.
- If it is necessary to peel fruit or vegetables that go brown in the air, sprinkle them with lemon juice or salad dressing straight away to stop them discolouring.
- Mix your own wholesome salad dressings and toss the salad in them at the last minute.
- If your dressing does not go far enough, thin it down with a little warm water.
- Never keep cut onions or garlic, they will lose their flavour and turn bitter. Besides, they form an ideal incubator for bacteria.
- Use as little salt as possible, use more fresh herbs instead.

Tips on serving salads

Almost all vegetables can be eaten raw, whether they are tubers, roots or leaves. The important thing is that you should buy what is in season. Many vegetables are, of course, available out of season because they are forced in a greenhouse or imported. However, it is always better to buy what is in season, because it is cheaper, it tastes better and it is more nutritious.

Preparing salads calls for imagination in

discovering new combinations of vegetables. The recipes in this section will give you lots of ideas of your own to experiment with.

If you are expecting guests, it is a good idea to leave the prepared raw vegetables undressed and to offer a selection of three or four different dressings for them to choose from (see pages 63-64).

Suggestions for salad combinations
Kohlrabi goes well with oranges, and also with green and red peppers. Kohlrabi and carrots taste good with a sweet cream dressing, and with a sharp vinegar dressing.

Celeriac combines well with pears, apples, nuts and cream.

Carrots go with cress, green and red peppers and sweetcorn in a savoury salad; or nuts, apples and cream in a sweet one.

Beetroot is lovely with horseradish and apples, with either cream or oil and vinegar.

Lettuce goes with almost anything, including a huge range of dressings (see page 63).

Chicory is good with oranges, mandarins, apples and cream, or with peppers, onions, oil and vinegar.

Endives can be made very piquant, but also taste good with a delicate lemon and honey dressing.

Cauliflower is excellent with nuts and cream. Pound the nuts into a pulp and mix them into the cream.

Cucumber goes well with cress and various different herbs, dressed with oil and vinegar; or with cream, lemon juice and honey.

White cabbage can be blanched by immersing briefly in boiling water, then dressed with cream or vinaigrette spiced with cumin.

Fresh herbs, chopped nuts, sesame seeds, sprouting seeds and cracked grain enhance any salad. You can also use the flowers of many culinary herbs, such as borage, dill and sage, not to mention many plants growing wild in the fields and hedgerows.

Spinach Salad with Chopped Egg

140 kcal   560 kJ

About 4oz (100g) spinach leaves
1 small onion

For the dressing
1 hard-boiled egg
2 dessertspoons fresh cream (30 per cent fat)
1 teaspoon mustard
1-2 dessertspoons wine vinegar
Sea salt
Freshly ground black pepper
Chopped chives

Wash the spinach leaves very thoroughly, discard the tough stalks and cut the leaves into strips about 1 inch (2cm) wide. Peel and chop the onion. Separate the yolk from the white of the egg. Mash the yolk with the cream, mustard and vinegar, season with salt, yeast and pepper and sprinkle with chives. Chop the egg white. Dress the salad with the sauce and garnish with the egg white.

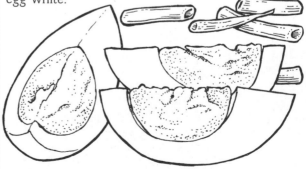

Tomato Salad with Mozzarella

Wash and slice the tomatoes and slice the cheese. Arrange them in layers in a deep plate and garnish with basil. Dribble oil and vinegar over the salad and season with salt and pepper, freshly ground for preference.

220 kcal   880 kJ

1-2 firm tomatoes
1-2oz (25-50g)
Mozzarella cheese
3 leaves of basil
1 dessertspoon wine
vinegar
1 dessertspoon cold-
pressed olive oil
Sea salt
Freshly ground black
pepper

Cucumber Salad with Roquefort Dressing

Wash the cucumber and radishes and slice them finely. Wash and chop the chives. Cream the cheese with the hot water. Mix in the lemon juice and oil and season with salt, peper and Cayenne. Stir the cucumber and radishes into the dressing until they are coated, and sprinkle with chives.

250 kcal   1000 kJ

¼ cucumber
5 radishes
Chives

For the dressing
1-2oz (25-50g) Roquefort
cheese
2 dessertspoons hot
water
½ dessertspoon lemon
juice
1 dessertspoon cold-
pressed sunflower oil
Sea salt
Freshly ground black
pepper
Cayenne pepper

170 kcal   680 kJ

Raw Carrot Salad with Nuts

1-2 medium carrots
Juice of half an orange
3 dessertspoons fresh
cream
A pinch of sea salt
A little honey (optional)
A few slices fresh ginger
1 teaspoon coarsely
chopped hazelnuts

Wash and peel or scrub the carrots. Grate them and mix with the remaining ingredients.

120 kcal   480 kJ

Piquant Dandelion Salad

1 bunch freshly picked
dandelion leaves
3-4 radishes

For the dressing
½ carton soured cream
1 teaspoon very sharp
mustard
½ teaspoon honey
1 dessertspoon lemon
juice
Sea salt
Paprika pepper
Finely chopped tarragon
leaves

Wash the dandelion leaves and drain them well. Wash and slice the radishes. Mix together all the ingredients for the dressing. Reserve some of the radish slices for garnish. Toss the salad in the sauce and garnish with remaining radish slices.

Kohlrabi and Carrot Salad

150 kcal   600 kJ

Wash and peel the kohlrabi and carrot and cut into very thin strips. Make the dressing and toss the vegetables in it.

½ **medium kohlrabi**
1 **carrot**

For the dressing
1 **dessertspoon wine vinegar**
1 **dessertspoon cold-pressed sunflower oil**
1 **clove of garlic, crushed**
½ **teaspoon mustard**
Sea salt
Freshly ground black pepper
A few chopped basil leaves

Cabbage Salad with Pineapple

200 kcal   800 kJ

Put the cabbage in a dish. Cut the pineapple into small pieces. Combine the cabbage and pineapple with the wine or lemon juice, honey and oil. Let it stand for a while so that the flavours mingle before eating.

6oz (150g) **grated white cabbage**
2 **slices pineapple**
2 **dessertspoons white wine or lemon juice**
½ **teaspoon honey**
1 **dessertspoon cold-pressed walnut oil**

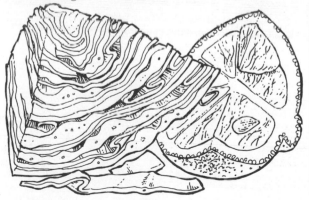

Bean Salad with Apple

200 kcal 800 kJ

About 3oz (80g) dried
haricot beans
About 2 pints (1 litre)
water
1 small apple
1 red pepper
1 teaspoon green
peppercorns
1-2 dessertspoons
sesame seeds, lightly
toasted without fat (for
garnish)

For the dressing
½ carton soured cream
Juice of half a lemon
Sea salt
Paprika pepper

(Makes two servings.)

Soak the beans in the water overnight. Cook for
about 40 minutes, drain and allow to cool. Wash
the apple and cut it with its peel into thin strips.
Wash and finely slice the red pepper. Mix the
beans with the apple, red pepper and
peppercorns. Combine the cream with the lemon
juice and season with salt and paprika. Toss the
salad in the dressing and sprinkle over the
sesame seeds.

Celery Cocktail

300 kcal 1200 kJ

½ head young celery
1 peach
1 dessertspoon lemon
juice
1 dessertspoon walnut
oil
Freshly ground black
pepper
2oz (50g) low fat white
cheese (fromage frais)
Flat-leaved parsley

Trim and wash the celery and cut it into pieces
about 1cm long. Immerse the peach briefly in
boiling water, skin it and cut into eight. Make
alternate layers of celery and peach in a small
dish, spoon over the lemon juice and oil and
season with pepper. Crumble the fresh cheese
over and garnish with parsley. This makes a
wonderful supper with freshly baked wholemeal
rolls.

Note: Steam the rest of the celery, sprinkle with
grated cheese and bake in the oven for supper
the next evening.

Lentil Salad with Leeks

(Makes two servings.)

Soak the lentils in the water overnight, then cook them for 30-40 minutes. Meanwhile peel and dice the carrot. Ten minutes before the end of the cooking time, add the carrot to the lentils. Drain the vegetables and let them cool. Peel and chop the onion. Wash the leek and slice it finely. Mix the leek and onion with the lentils and carrots. Make the dressing and stir it into the vegetables. Let the flavours mingle for a while, then sprinkle with parsley.

220 kcal   880 kJ

About 3oz (80g) dried lentils
About 2 pints (1 litre) water
1 carrot
1 medium onion
1 small leek

For the dressing
2 dessertspoons wine vinegar
1 teaspoon mustard
2 dessertspoons cold-pressed sunflower oil
Sea salt
Fresh ground black pepper
Parsley for garnish

Potato Salad with Chives and Radishes

(Makes two meals.)

Wash the potatoes and boil for about 20 minutes. Let them cool, then peel and slice them. Wash the radishes, trim and slice half of them and leave the rest for the second meal. Mix the sliced radishes with the peeled, chopped onion and the potatoes.

Make the dressing and mix into the salad.

If you eat half the salad for your evening meal, store the rest, tightly sealed, in the fridge to take to work the next day, mixed with the remaining radishes.

190 kcal   760 kJ

About 1lb (400-500g) potatoes
1 bunch of radishes
1 small onion

For the dressing
2 dessertspoons vinegar
2-3 dessertspoons cold-pressed vegetable oil
2 dessertspoons hot water
Sea salt
Freshly ground black pepper
Chopped chives

Ceps Salad

200 kcal   800 kJ

(Ceps are wild mushrooms (yellow boletus). They can be bought dried, in which case they should be soaked for a minute or two in water (or milk) and rinsed well before use.)

About 6oz (150g) freshly gathered ceps (or use dried ceps)
1 cup of water
A few walnuts
1 tomato

Trim and wash the ceps and cook them in a little water for about 5 minutes. Drain and slice them. Make the dressing.

For the dressing
1-2 dessertspoons lemon juice or wine vinegar
½ teaspoon mustard
1-2 dessertspoons walnut oil
Sea salt
Freshly ground black pepper

Chop the walnuts. Immerse the tomato briefly in boiling water, skin it, deseed it and chop it. Mix all the ingredients together well.

Seeds and Sprouts

Seeds and sprouts are growing in popularity because they taste delicious and they are easily digestible and extremely nutritious.

The germination process begins with the intake of water and oxygen. Enzymes trigger a chain reaction that causes an enormous increase in vitamin content, especially in the B group vitamins.

It costs very little to germinate seeds. You do not need much space either, which makes it ideal for the one-person household. And the best of it is that you can produce exactly the amount of fresh food you need, all year round. This is, of course, particularly useful in the winter when herbs are scarce.

The first requirement is good quality seeds. Then you need a glass jar, an elastic band and a piece of muslin or nylon net. The seeds are first soaked very thoroughly and then kept moist in their little 'greenhouse' until they germinate.

You can also buy germination boxes, which have several tiers for seeds and are specially designed to produce the optimum light and moisture conditions for germination.

The most important thing, though, is that your seeds are healthy, untreated and in top condition for germination.

The characteristics of germination differ according to the seed.

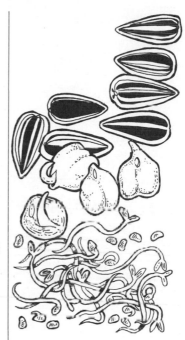

Small seeds

This group includes **lucerne**, **mustard**, **sesame** and **radish**. They grow very quickly and are ready to eat as soon as the first few tiny leaves have formed. Sometimes small seeds are available in mixed packets.

Radish seeds are particularly useful because they help prevent the growth of bacteria, yeasts and mould. Sprinkle these sprouting seeds on a salad for a very piquant taste. You will find you need almost no salt.

Grains

Grains include **Wheat, rye, barley** and **oats**. These cereals develop a sweet nutty taste during germination. Dress and eat them on their own, sprinkle them over other salads or eat them in muesli.

Other seeds suitable for germinating are **pulses,** (**soya bean** sprouts are probably the best known), **sunflower seeds** (which taste excellent), and seeds with lubricating properties such as **linseed** and **cress**.

How to germinate seeds

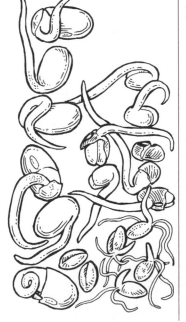

First rinse the seeds thoroughly. Put them into the glass jar or germinating box. Cover them with three times their own volume of water (preferably still mineral water). Leave them to soak for six to eight hours.

Pour off the water, rinse the seeds and remove any that have not swollen. Cover the jar with muslin, or put the lid on the box. Stand it on a tilt so that excess water drains off and air can circulate freely round the seeds. The best temperature for germination is about 21°C. Rinse the seeds in fresh water twice a day. Hygiene is important to prevent the formation of mould.

Within a few days, the seeds will sprout and be ready to eat.

Remember
- The seeds should be kept moist, but not wet.
- They should be rinsed regularly.
- They should have enough room to grow.
- The temperature should be kept stable.

Colourful Sprouting Salad

130 kcal   520 kJ

Buy a whole bunch of radishes and use the rest as snacks for the office. Wash the shallot, tomato and radishes and slice them finely. Make the dressing with the lemon juice, oil, mustard, and mix it in with the sprouts and vegetables.

These sprouts also go very well with lamb's lettuce, endives and chicory.

1-2 dessertspoons mixed alfalfa and radish seeds, sprouted
1 shallot
1 tomato
5 radishes

For the dressing
1 teaspoon lemon juice
1-2 teaspoons olive oil
2 teaspoons mustard
A little honey
Sea salt
Freshly ground black pepper

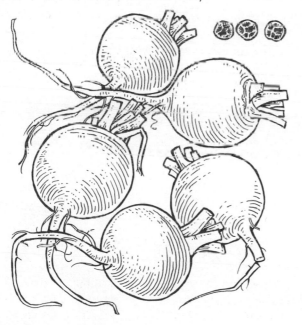

Mushroom and Cress Salad

100 kcal   400 kJ

5oz (125g) fresh
mushrooms
1 teaspoon lemon juice
1 medium tomato
½ cup sprouted cress
seeds

For the dressing
2 dessertspoons fresh
cream
Sea salt
Freshly ground black
pepper

Trim, wash and clice the mushrooms. Sprinkle
them with lemon juice. Wash and quarter the
tomato. Make the dressing and mix all the
ingredients together.

Beetroot and Sprouted Wheat Salad

220 kcal   880 kJ

1 small beetroot, cooked
1 small onion
2 dessertspoons wheat
seeds, sprouted
1 dessertspoon cold-
pressed walnut oil
1 dessertspoon lemon
juice
Freshly ground black
pepper
Sea salt

Peel the beetroot, cut it into four and then slice it
thinly. Peel the onion and cut it into rings. Mix
the beetroot and onion with the sprouted wheat.
Make a dressing with the oil, lemon juice, pepper
and salt and pour it over the salad.

Lentil Sprout and Apple Salad

100 kcal   400 kJ

Peel the apple, grate it coarsely and mix with the sprouted lentils. Make a dressing with the cream, lemon juice, pepper, salt and honey. Mix all the ingredients together and garnish with lemon balm leaves.

1 medium apple
½ cup lentils, sprouted

For the dressing
2 dessertspoons fresh cream (30 per cent fat)
1 dessertspoon lemon juice
Freshly ground black pepper
Sea salt
½ teaspoon honey
Few lemon blam leaves (for garnish)

Quark Dip with Sprouted Seeds

180 kcal   720 kJ

Rinse the sprouts thoroughly and mix them with the quark, a little milk, the yeast extract, pepper, honey and Cayenne. Check the seasoning. Eat half for supper and take the rest to work for lunch the next day. Use it as a dip for carrot sticks, slices of cucumber and strips of red pepper. Can be prepared in advance.

3-4 dessertspoons sprouted seeds (alfalfa or radish)
8oz quark (20 per cent fat)
A little milk
1 teaspoon yeast extract
Freshly ground black pepper
½ teaspoon honey
Cayenne pepper

250 kcal   1000 kJ

1 head of chicory
2 dessertspoons soya
bean sprouts

For the dressing
½ ripe banana
½ carton soured cream
(10 per cent fat)
1 dessertspoon lemon
juice
Sea salt
A pinch of ground
ginger
½ teaspoon curry
powder
½ teaspoon honey
1 teaspoon chopped
parsley

Chicory and Beansprouts in Curried Cream

Wash the chicory, halve it lengthways and remove the bitter heart. Cut the leaves crossways into strips. Mix the chicory with the bean sprouts.

Mash or purée the banana and mix it with the rest of the ingredients for the dressing. Pour the dressing over the salad and garnish with parsley.

200 kcal   800 kJ

About 5oz (125g) grapes
5oz (125g) white
cabbage
2 dessertspoons
sprouted wheat

For the dressing
2 dessertspoons fresh
cream
1 teaspoon cold-pressed
walnut oil
1 dessert spoon soya
sauce
1 teaspoon lemon juice
A pinch of ginger
Freshly ground black
pepper
1 dessertspoon chopped
flat-leaved parsley

Sweet Sour Sprouting Salad

Wash the grapes well, halve them and remove the pips. Chop the cabbage and mix it with the grapes and sprouted wheat.

Combine the ingredients for the dressing, stir it into the salad and leave, covered, until the flavours have mingled well. This salad tastes good with other sprouted grains, too. It makes an ideal packed lunch.

Mung Beansprout Spread with Garlic

Mix all the ingredients together. This tastes good on wholemeal bread or rolls.

120 kcal   480 kJ

½ cup mung beansprouts
1 small onion
1 clove of garlic
A few sprigs of dill
2-3 dessertspoons quark (20 per cent fat)
A little milk (optional)
Sea salt

Sauces — Hot and Cold

Sauces, like herbs, should not mask the flavour of a dish. They should lift it, enhance it and round it off.

In this section you will find suggestions for delicious, easily prepared sauces to be served hot or cold.

Basic Recipe for Hot Sauces

130 kcal   520 kJ per serving

Mix the flour and oil together in a small saucepan. Pour over the stock or milk and cook gently, stirring, until the cause is smooth and thick. Season and stir in the cream.

Using this basic method you can prepare various different sauces. If you always make enough sauce for two servings, you can flavour each portion differently. If a skin forms on the sauce after it has stood for a while, simply stir it back in.

2 dessertspoons cold-pressed vegetable oil
1-2 dessertspoons fine-ground wholemeal flour,sieved if liked
1½ cups vegetable stock (homemade or from a bouillon cube) or milk
Sea salt
1-2 dessertspoons fresh cream

Variations

Herb sauce
Add 2 dessertspoons finely chopped or snipped herbs (such as dill, parsley or chives) and season with a little lemon juice.

Caper sauce
Stir in 1 dessertspoon chopped capers and the yolk of an egg. Add a squeeze of lemon juice.

Mustard sauce
Add 1 dessertspoon mild mustard and a few
drops of vinegar. Round the sauce off with a little
honey if liked.

Curried mango sauce
Stir in ½ teaspoon curry powder and 1
dessertspoon chopped mango chutney.

Horseradish sauce
Stir in 1 dessertspoon grated horseradish and a
little honey.

Cheese sauce
Stir in 2 dessertspoons grated cheese, season
with nutmeg and add a little white wine to taste.

Apple Cream Sauce

190 kcal   760 kJ

1 small apple
½ carton soured cream
2-3 dessertspoons fresh
cream
1 dessertspoon currants
1 teaspoon honey

Peel the apple and grate it coarsely. Mix the
soured cream with the fresh cream. Stir in the
currants, honey and apple. Mix well.
   Try this sauce with waffles and potato puffs.

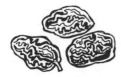

Mushroom Sauce

160 kcal   640 kJ

Trim and slice the mushrooms. Chop the shallot.
Cook them gently in the margarine. Season with
salt and pepper and sprinkle over the lemon
juice. Stir in the cream and add the parsley.

This sauce goes very well with noodles, millet,
rice, cauliflower or aubergines.

6oz (150g) fresh
mushrooms
1 shallot
⅓oz (10g) soft vegetable
margarine
Freshly ground black
pepper
Sea salt
1 dessertspoon lemon
juice
3-4 dessertspoons fresh
cream
3 dessertspoons
chopped parsley

Tomato Sauce with Basil

150 kcal   600 kJ

Immerse the tomatoes briefly in boiling water.
Peel and chop them. Heat the olive oil in a pan
and crush the garlic into it. Add the tomatoes,
stir and cook for a few minutes. Add the tomato
purée, salt, pepper and cream. Sprinkle on the
fresh basil. This sauce tastes excellent with
noodles and rice dishes.

2 very ripe beef
tomatoes
1 dessertspoon olive oil
1 clove of garlic
1 dessertspoon tomato
purée
Sea salt
Freshly ground black
pepper
2 dessertspoons cream
(optional)
Fresh basil, finely
chopped, to taste

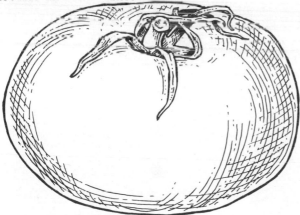

Spinach Cream Sauce

180 kcal   720 kJ

About 4oz (100g) fresh
spinach
A small bunch of chervil
Sea salt
Nutmeg
2 dessertspoons soured
cream

Wash the spinach and leave water clinging to it.
Cook it for a few minutes without adding extra
water. Purée the cooked spinach with the chervil,
salt, nutmeg and cream, in a liquidizer if you
have one.

Serve this sauce with jacket potatoes, potatoes
in foil, or pancakes.

Garlic Sauce

180 kcal   720 kJ

1 carton live yogurt or
soured cream
Sea salt
Freshly ground black
pepper
A very little honey
3 cloves garlic, crushed
1 dessertspoon chopped
dill

(This sauce should be eaten straightaway.)

Mix all the ingredients together well. This sauce
can be eaten with raw vegetables to dip into it
and wholemeal rolls.

Green Sauce

250 kcal   1000 kJ

1 carton live yogurt or
soured cream
1 teaspoon mustard
2-3 dessertspoons
chopped herbs (chervil,
sorrel, dill, parsley,
borage)
Freshly ground black
pepper
Sea salt
1 dessertspoon lemon
juice
1 hard-boiled egg

Stir all the ingredients together with a little
crushed ice.

This sauce goes with all kinds of vegetable
dishes, and with new potatoes in their skins or
potatoes in foil.

Sauces and Dressings for Salads and Vegetable Dishes

These sauces can be prepared in advance and kept, covered, in the fridge for a few days.

Vinaigrette dressing

Mix all the ingredients together thoroughly. According to taste, you can also add chopped herbs, finely chopped onion or, even better, shallot or crushed garlic.

1-2 dessertspoons wine vinegar
Sea salt
A little honey
4-5 dessertspoons oil
Freshly ground black pepper

Tarragon Dressing

Mix all the ingredients together thoroughly.

1-2 dessertspoons wine vinegar or 2 3 dessertspoons lemon juice
Sea salt
White pepper
4-5 dessertspoons oil
A few tarragon leaves

1-2 egg yolks
1 teaspoon mustard
Sea salt
A little honey
4-6 dessertspoons oil

Basic Mayonnaise Recipe

All the ingredients should be at room temperature. Whisk together the egg yolks, mustard, salt and honey (this should be done by hand). Then, still whisking, add the oil a drop at a time. Keep in a cool place.

Mayonnaise can be prepared in advance. For a less rich low-fat sauce, mix mayonnaise with yogurt.

Mayonnaise can be used on many salads and goes particularly well with leaf salads, cabbage, cucumber and radishes.

Basic mayonnaise
1 dessertspoon finely chopped onion
1-2 dessertspoons finely chopped herbs
1 dessertspoon capers
Green peppercorns
1 teaspoon sharp mustard
1 hard-boiled egg, finely chopped

Sauce Remoulade

Mix the ingredients together and use as a dip for raw vegetables.

Try soured cream or yogurt instead of egg yolk and oil.

Basic mayonnaise
1 dessertspoon mango chutney
1 teaspoon curry powder

Curried Mayonnaise

Mix all the ingredients together. This dressing goes well with Chinese leaves and chicory.

Cream Sauce with Fresh Herbs

Mix the ingredients together and use on almost any salad.

1 carton soured cream
Juice of half a lemon
Sea salt
½ teaspoon apple juice concentrate
Freshly ground black pepper
2 dessertspoons chopped herbs

Walnut Sauce

Mix the ingredients together. Tastes especially good with carrots, fennel and white cabbage.

If you want your salad dressings to be less rich and lower in cholesterol, use soured cream or yogurt instead of egg yolk and oil. Make sure you have stirred the cream first so that it is smooth and not lumpy before you add the other ingredients.

1 carton soured cream or yogurt
Juice of ½-1 lemon
Sea salt
1 teaspoon honey
A pinch of ginger
1-2 dessertspoons coarsely chopped walnuts

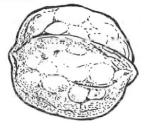

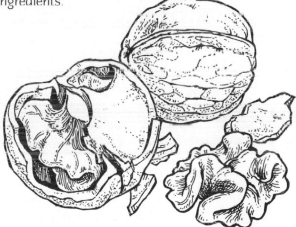

Healthy Soups

Well prepared and nourishing soups are ideal for the single person, because they can be made in advance and frozen for future use.

The basis for most of these recipes is a good vegetable stock that you can prepare yourself from green vegetables, potatoes, parsley roots, celery, leeks, onions and carrots. Add a bayleaf, salt and pepper and parsley leaves. Even vegetable peelings and trimmings add goodness and flavour. Vegetable stock can be enriched with yeast extract. It will keep for several days in the fridge.

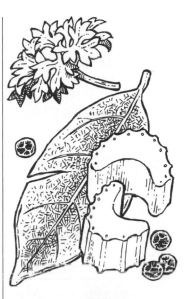

Vegetable Soup with Poached Egg

(Makes two servings.)

Trim, wash and chop the vegetables. Put them in the stock, bring to the boil and simmer for about 10 minutes. Season to taste with salt, pepper and coriander.

Meanwhile, bring a small pan of water to the boil, add the vinegar and a little salt. Break the egg into a ladle and slide it carefully into the boiling water. Poach for 3-4 minutes.

Pour half the soup into a deep soup plate, add the egg and sprinkle with parsley or sprouted seeds.

Allow the rest of the soup to cool and eat it the next day with fresh herbs and grated cheese.

180 kcal   720 kJ

About 500g vegetables (such as cauliflower, carrots, leeks, kohlrabi – any leftovers from the day before)
4-5 cups vegetable stock
Sea salt
Freshly ground black pepper
Crushed coriander
1 dessertspoon vinegar
1 dessertspoon chopped parsley or sprouted seeds
2 pints (1 litre) water
1 egg

Onion Soup

130 kcal   520 kJ

⅓ oz (10g) soft vegetable
margarine
1 medium onion
2 cups vegetable stock
1 bayleaf
Juniper berries
Peppercorns
Sea salt
2-3 dessertspoons white
wine

Peel the onion and it into rings. Fry them gently
in the fat, then pour over the vegetable stock.
Add the bayleaf, juniper berries and peppercorns
and simmer for 10-15 minutes. Season to taste
with sea salt and white wine.

Baked Onion Soup

220 kcal   880 kJ

Onion soup (see
previous recipe)
1 slice of wholemeal
bread
1 slice of cheese
Paprika pepper

Pour the soup into an ovenproof dish. Toast the
bread and float it on the soup. Lay the cheese on
the bread. Bake in the oven at 200°C (400°F,
Gas Mark 6) for about 10 minutes, or put under
a hot grill until the cheese is bubbling and
golden.

Cabbage Soup

140 kcal   560 kJ

½ white cabbage
1 onion
2-3 potatoes
1 bayleaf
Freshly ground black
pepper
Sea salt
Cumin
3-4 cups vegetable stock
1 teaspoon butter
1 clove garlic, crushed
1 dessertspoon chopped
parsley

(Makes two portions; freeze one.)

Trim and chop the cabbage. Store the other half,
well sealed, in the fridge. Peel and dice the onion
and potato. Put the vegetables in the stock,
season with pepper, salt and cumin and simmer
for 15-20 minutes. Add butter, garlic and
chopped parsley to taste.
    (Use the rest of the cabbage in a salad.)

Potato Soup

See potato recipes, page 98.

Cold Cucumber Soup

80 kcal 320 kJ

Swirl the quark into the vegetable stock. Wash the cucumber, cut off the end and grate it coarsely. Stir the cucumber and garlic into the stock. Season with salt, pepper and Cayenne. Wash the dill, chop or snip it finely and sprinkle over the soup. Eat with a slice of wholemeal toast spread with garlic butter.

2 dessertspoons quark (20 per cent fat)
½ pint (300 ml) vegetable stock or water, with 1 teaspoon yeast extract added
¼ cucumber (eat the rest in salad)
1 clove garlic, crushed
Sea salt
White pepper
Cayenne pepper
A small bunch of dill

Nettle Soup with Cream

100 kcal 400 kJ

Peel the onion and chop it finely. Cook gently in the hot fat until transparent. Pour over the stock. Wash and chop the nettles and add to the soup. Cook for a few minutes and season with salt, mace and cream to taste.

1 small onion
1 teaspoon butter or soft vegetable margarine
Generous ½ pint (300-400ml) vegetable stock
1 bunch fresh nettles
Sea salt
Mace
2 dessertspoons fresh cream

150 kcal   600 kJ

3-4 medium, ripe
tomatoes
1-2 cups vegetable stock
½ red pepper (eat the
rest in a salad)
¼ cucumber (eat the
rest in a salad)
1 small onion
1 clove of garlic, crushed
(optional)
Celery salt
Cayenne pepper
2 dessertspoons olive oil
2-3 dessertspoons lemon
juice
2 dessertspoons
chopped chives

Gazpacho

(Makes two servings.)

Immerse the tomatoes briefly in boiling water,
then peel them. Dice or purée them and add to
the stock. Chop the red pepper, cucumber and
onion very finely and add to the soup. Then add
the garlic, celery salt, Cayenne pepper, olive oil
and lemon juice to taste and sprinkle with
chopped chives.

Eat this soup with fresh bread and butter. Take
the second helping to work for your lunch.

140 kcal   520 kJ

3 carrots
2 cups vegetable stock
Coriander
Sea salt
White pepper
Chopped chervil
2-3 dessertspoons cream
1 teaspoon sunflower
seeds or chopped
hazelnuts

Cream of Carrot Soup

Chop the carrots finely and cook in the vegetable
stock for about 15 minutes. Blend or purée in a
liquidizer. Add coriander, salt, pepper, cream and
chervil to taste, then sprinkle with the sunflower
seeds or nuts.

Pearl Barley Soup

(Makes four servings; freeze three.)

Soak the barley overnight. Heat the margarine in a pan. Chop the onion, leek and carrot and fry gently until soft. Pour over the pearl barley and the water in which it has been soaking. Season with salt, pepper and nutmeg. Simmer for 30-40 minutes. Sprinkle with parsley.

Always add fresh herbs to defrosted soup.

150 kcal   600 kJ

¾oz (20g) soft vegetable margarine
1 medium onion
1 small leek
1 medium carrot
3-4oz (80-100g) pearl barley
2 pints (1 litre) water
Sea salt
Freshly ground black pepper
Nutmeg
Chopped parsley

Cracked Wheat Broth

Toast the cracked wheat lightly in a hot pan without fat. You can prepare more than the quantity indicated and use the rest in muesli. Trim, wash and slice the leek. Add it to the stock and simmer for about 15 minutes. Stir in the wheat and season with pepper, marjoram and parsley.

100 kcal   400 kJ

2 dessertspoons cracked wheat
1 leek
2 cups vegetable stock
Freshly ground black pepper
Marjoram
Freshly chopped parsley

Hotpots

You can make delicious hotpots which you can freeze till you need them, or you can make enough for two meals and serve them differently. A hotpot makes a hearty meal on its own, but the addition of more stock turns it into a good soup. Hotpots are easy to make, so they are a useful and versatile alternative for a small household.

Always use the freshest possible ingredients. If fresh vegetables in season are not available, use frozen vegetables, preferably organically grown ones that you have frozen yourself. Always use natural wholemeal products and add fresh herbs after cooking.

Try to keep cooking times as short as possible and use pots with tightly fitting lids. Never keep food warm for any length of time. Let it cool and heat it up a second time to minimize loss of vitamins.

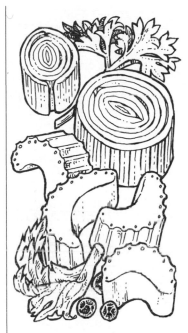

Gardener's Vegetable Hotpot

(Makes two meals.)

Trim, wash and dice or slice the vegetables. Put them all in a pot, pour over the water, add the yeast extract and simmer for about 15 minutes. Season to taste.

Divide the hotpot into two portions. Allow one to cool and then freeze it. Add the chopped parsley and the butter to the other portion.

250 kcal   1000 kJ

1 medium potato
2 medium carrots
½ small head of celery with leaves
1 small leek
1 small kohlrabi
1 small onion
1½ pints (750ml) water
1 teaspoon yeast extract
Sea salt
Freshly ground black pepper
Cumin
1 bunch flat-leaved parsley
⅓oz (10g) butter

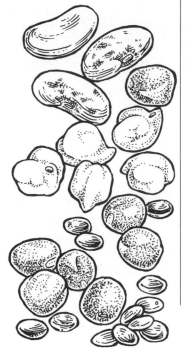

Pulses are an ideal addition to hotpots. They are an important ingredient in wholefood cooking, being rich in protein, vitamins, minerals and, of course, fibre. They have a higher fibre content than any other vegetable, which makes them as satisfying as they are nourishing.

In some parts of the world beans (mainly soya beans), peas and lentils are the staple foods and often the only source of protein.

Pulses need to be cooked for a fairly long time. They cannot be eaten raw, except when they have been germinated (see page 52). To minimize cooking time, pulses should be soaked for several hours in cold water until they have plumped up. They will still need to be cooked for between forty minutes and one hour depending on their age. A pressure cooker cuts this time almost in half. Old beans take a very long time to swell up and cannot be cooked easily.

Butter Beans with Cheese

(Makes two portions.)

Soak the beans overnight or even longer. Cook them in the water they have soaked in (decide on the quantity of water according to how thick you want the dish to be), with the bayleaf and diced vegetables for about an hour over a low heat. When the beans are soft, remove the skins as these are not easily digested. Season to taste and divide the hotpot into two portions. Sprinkle one with cheese and parsely and freeze the other.

290 kcal   1160 kJ
About 4oz (100g) butter beans
½-1 pint (300-600ml) water
1 small leek
1 small carrot
1 small onion
1 bayleaf
1 vegetable stock cube
Sea salt
Freshly ground black pepper
Cayenne pepper
Nutmeg
1 clove garlic, crushed (optional)
1 dessertspoon grated cheese
1 dessertspoon chopped parsley

Lentil Hotpot

(Makes two servings.)

Soak the lentils overnight, then bring them to the boil in the water they have soaked in.
Meanwhile, trim and wash the greens, potatoes, onion and carrot. Slice the greens, peel and chop the rest of the vegetables. Add the vegetables to the lentils and cook over a low heat for about 50 minutes. Season to taste and divide the hotpot into two. Serve one portion in a deep soup plate, garnished with cream and parsley, and freeze the other when cool.

280 kcal   1180 kJ
3-4oz (80-100g) lentils
1 bunch of greens
2 medium potatoes
1 medium onion
1 carrot
1 pint (600ml) water
3 dessertspoons red wine
1 teaspoon yeast extract
Thyme
Freshly ground black pepper
Sea salt
1 dessertspoon buttermilk or soured cream
1 dessertspoon chopped parsley

Soya Bean Hotpot

280 kcal   1120 kJ

(Makes two meals.)

3-4oz (80-100g) soya beans
1 pint (600ml) water
1 teaspoon yeast extract
⅓oz (10g) soft vegetable margarine
1 medium onion
1 clove garlic
2 medium carrots
1 small head of celery
Dried mixed herbs
Fresh sage
Sea salt
Freshly ground black pepper
1 dessertspoon chopped chives

Soak the soya beans overnight. Drain and simmer in fresh water with the yeast extract for 50-60 minutes.

Meanwhile, chop the onion and garlic. Heat the margarine in a pan and cook the onion and garlic until transparent. Peel and dice the carrot and slice the celery, and add them to the pan with a little water. Cook for about 15 minutes. Add the vegetables to the beans with the herbs and season to taste with salt and pepper. Divide the hotpot into two, freeze one portion and sprinkle the other with chives.

Vegetable Dishes

As we have already seen from the chapter on salads, vegetables are an important source of essential nutrients. Besides water and carbohydrates (for energy), they provide us with vitamins; minerals; trace elements; fibre; natural colourings and flavourings – and there may be other valuable substances that have not yet been discovered.

Today vegetables do not just come from individual growers. They are produced by intensive cultivation on a large scale. Growers are aiming for a high yield and perfect looking specimens. In order to achieve this, they treat the soil and their plants with fertilizers and pesticides. These substances are absorbed by the vegetables and can be dangerous if they are taken into the human body in large quantities. The most commonly used substances are nitrates. These are used to fertilize the soil and are found in varying quantities in many vegetables. They are most highly concentrated in greenhouse-grown lettuce; next comes spinach, beetroot, celery and radishes.

Environmental poisons such as lead, cadmium and mercury are also found in many vegetables, especially those grown near roads with heavy traffic. Traces of harmful pesticides also remain in the plants.

These are good reasons for buying all your vegetables from farms which use organic methods. Even then, there is no guarantee that they will be absolutely pure, but the presence of harmful substances will have been kept to a minimum.

Careful shopping for healthy produce should be backed up by the careful preparation of the vegetables, to ensure that as few nutrients as possible are lost. Short cooking times will help the vegetables keep their colour, taste and a certain amount of bite.

Cooking Methods

There are several methods of cooking vegetables.

Blanching. Prepared vegetables are immersed in boiling water for two or three minutes, then plunged into cold water or held under cold, running water. This is a preliminary method of cooking. The cooking liquor can be stored in the fridge and used as a base for soups.

Sweating. Prepared vegetables are set over a gentle heat in a tightly closed pan with a very little water and/or fat. Some vegetables (such as spinach) can be cooked in only the water clinging to them after washing.

Steaming. Prepared vegetables are set over a pan of boiling water in a steamer.

Do not keep cooked vegetables hot for any length of time. Either eat them straight away or take them off the stove and put them in a cool place to be heated up again if necessary. This also applies when you make enough for two helpings. Allow the uneaten helping to cool, then cover it well and store in the fridge.

Artichoke Classic Style

130 kcal   520 kJ

1 artichoke
Salted water
1 lemon
Sauce of your choice
(see page 63)

Wash the artichoke well and cut off the stalk. Simmer in salted water, to which you have added a couple of slices of lemon, for about 30 minutes. The artichoke is cooked when one of the lower leaves will come away easily at a tug.
To eat the artichoke, put it on a plate, pull off the leaves one by one and dip them in the sauce. Suck off the tender flesh part of the leaf. Avoiding the choke, eat the heart with a knife

and fork and plenty of sauce.

This makes a very delicious starter if you are entertaining.

Fried Aubergine

150 kcal   600 kJ

Wash and slice the aubergine. Season with pepper, herbs and garlic. Fry in hot olive oil.

1 **aubergine (or half a large aubergine)**
Freshly ground black pepper
Dried mixed herbs
1 clove garlic, crushed
2 **dessertspoons olive oil**

Ratatouille

240 kcal   960 kJ

(Makes two servings.)

Cut the aubergine in half lengthwise. Dice the aubergine and courgettes. Cut the pepper in half, remove the pith and seeds and dice it. Dice the tomatoes. Peel and chop the onion and cook in olive oil until golden. Add the remaining ingredients and sweat over a low heat for about 15 minutes. Season to taste and sprinkle with parsley and grated cheese.

Eat this with risotto one day and with potato purée the next.

1 **aubergine**
2 **courgettes**
1 **green or red pepper**
2 **tomatoes**
1 **medium onion**
A **little olive oil**
1 clove garlic, crushed
Sea salt
Freshly ground black pepper
Chopped parsley
1 **dessertspoon grated cheese**

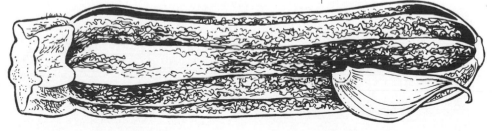

200 kcal   800 kJ

1 small cauliflower
1 dessertspoon lemon
juice
Sea salt
Vinaigrette dressing (see
page 63)

Cauliflower with Vinaigrette Dressing

Trim and wash the cauliflower and cook it whole in salted water with the lemon juice for 8-10 minutes. (It should still have bite when it is cooked.) Divide it into florets and toss in vinaigrette dressing. This dish tastes particularly good with new potatoes.

220 kcal   800 kJ

1 small cauliflower
1 dessertspoon lemon
juice
Sea salt
1 dessertspoon
wholemeal flour
2 dessertspoons cream
1 egg yolk (save the
white to put in an
omelette)
1oz (25g) Roquefort or
Gorgonzola cheese
Flat-leaved parsley

Cauliflower with Cream Cheese Sauce

Cook th cauliflower in salted water with the lemon juice for 8-10 minutes. (It should still have bite when cooked.)

Put the flour in a pan without fat. Heat it over a flame until it begins to small good. Pour on half a cup of cauliflower water and stir vigorously to prevent lumps forming. When it has thickened, remove from the heat and swirl in the cream and the egg yolk. Stir in the crumbled cheese and the chopped parsley.

Divide the cauliflower into florets and pour the sauce over it. Serve with rice.

Broccoli with Nut Butter

Wash the broccoli and sweat in a little water.
Add the salt, pepper and white wine. Mix the
butter with the hazelnuts and add to the
broccoli. Serve with buckwheat.

7-8oz (200-250g)
broccoli
Sea salt
Freshly ground black
pepper
2 dessertspoons dry
white wine
⅓oz (10g) butter
1 teaspoon coarsely
chopped hazelnuts

Green Beans with Garlic

160 kcal   640 kJ

Chop the onion. Sweat the onion and garlic in oil
until transparent. Wash and trim the beans, cut
them up if necessary and sweat for 10-15
minutes in a little water.

Immerse the tomato briefly in boiling water,
skin it, dice it and add it to the beans with the
onion and garlic. Season and serve hot, dotted
with butter if liked. This tastes good with baked
potatoes.

1 small onion
1 clove garlic, crushed
1 dessertspoon olive oil
7oz (200g) green beans
1 medium tomato
Freshly ground black
pepper

Variation
Instead of olive oil, garlic and tomatoes, serve
green beans with butter and diced pears.

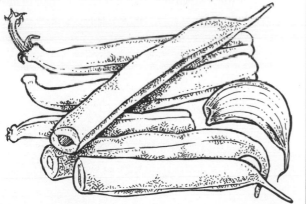

380 kcal   1520 kJ

1 small or half a large head of celery (use the rest in a salad)
½ cup rye grains (page 52)
3 dessertspoons fresh cream
1 egg
2 dessertspoons grated cheese
Nutmeg
Freshly ground black pepper
Sea salt
1 teaspoon chopped celery leaves

Baked Celery

Wash the celery and cut it into pieces about 1 inch (2cm) long. Sweat it in a little water for about 10 minutes. Drain and transfer to a greased ovenproof dish. Sprinkle on the rye. Mix the cream with the egg, cheese and seasoning and pour into the dish. Cook in a preheated oven for about 20 minutes. Sprinkle with celery leaves and serve with a green salad.

225 kcal   900 kJ

20-30 fresh mushroom caps
5oz (125g) wholewheat flour
½ teaspoon sea salt
Freshly ground black pepper
1 glass beer or milk
Vegetable oil for deep-frying

Beer-Flavoured Deep-Fried Mushrooms

Trim and wash the mushrooms. Mix the flour with the salt, pepper and beer, making sure that the batter is not too thin. Heat the oil in a deep pan. Dip the mushrooms in the batter and deep-fry them. Makes an excellent appetizer.

Mushrooms with Parsley

130 kcal   520 kJ

Trim the mushrooms, cutting off any soft stalks, wash them well and slice finely. Sprinkle with white wine or lemon juice. Sweat the onion in the margarine and add the mushrooms. Cook gently for about 10 minutes. Season with salt and pepper and sprinkle with parsley. Serve with creamed potato purée and salad.

About 8oz (250g) mushrooms
2 dessertspoons white wine or 1 dessertspoon lemon juice
⅓ oz (10g) soft vegetable margarine
1 small onion
Sea salt
White pepper
2 dessertspoons chopped parsley

Variation
Stir cream into the mushrooms.

Chicory with Desiccated Coconut

200 kcal   800 kJ

Trim and halve the chicory and remove the bitter centre. Sprinkle with lemon juice. Sweat with a very little water for 8-10 minutes. Season with salt and honey. Pour over the curry dressing and sprinkle with coconut. Serve with rice.

2 heads of chicory
2 dessertspoons lemon juice
Sea salt
1 teaspoon honey
Curry dressing (see page 64)
1 dessertspoon desiccated coconut, toasted without fat

Fennel with Wholemeal Breadcrumbs

200 kcal   800 kJ

Wash the fennel, reserve the leaves, cut the bulb in half and cook it in white wine or vegetable stock for 10-15 minutes. Season with a little salt. Heat the butter and brown the breadcrumbs in it. Add to the fennel.

1 fennel bulb
½ cup white wine or vegetable stock
Sea salt
1 dessertspoon butter
1 teaspoon wholemeal breadcrumbs

Variation
Sweat the fennel and add diced tomato, garlic and herbs.

Cucumber in Tomato Sauce

100 kcal   400 kJ

½ cucumber
1 dessertspoon tomato
purée
1 clove garlic, crushed
Sea salt
Freshly ground black
pepper
1 dessertspoon chopped
dill

Wash the cucumber well, cut it in half lengthways, then slice it. Sweat it in a little vegetable stock for about 8 minutes. Add the tomato purée, garlic, salt and pepper and continue to cook for a few minutes. Sprinkle with dill. Serve with millet or polenta.

Mushroom-Stuffed Kohlrabi

280 kcal   1120 kJ

1 medium kohlrabi
6oz (150g) fresh
mushrooms
1 medium onion
⅓oz (10g) soft vegetable
margarine
2 dessertspoons soured
cream
Sea salt
Freshly ground black
pepper
1 teaspoon tomato purée
Flat-leaved parsley

Peel the kohlrabi carefully, and cut off a 'lid'. Scoop out the centre and put to one side. Cook the kohlrabi and its 'lid' in lightly salted water for about 10 minutes. Meanwhile, chop the scooped-out inside of the vegetable. Trim, wash and slice the mushrooms. Peel and dice the onion and sweat in hot fat until transparent. Add the mushrooms and chopped kohlrabi and cook for about 10 minutes, until the liquid has evaporated. Stir in the remaining ingredients. Stuff the kohlrabi with this mixture and serve with brown rice or potato purée.

Buttered Kohlrabi

120 kcal   480 kJ

1-2 kohlrabi
A little vegetable stock
1 dessertspoon butter
White pepper
Fresh coriander

Peel the kohlrabi and chop the leaves. Cut it in half, then slice it and sweat it in a little vegetable stock for about 10 minutes. Add the remaining ingredients and sprinkle with the chopped coriander leaves.

Leeks and Carrots

(Makes two meals.)

120 kcal   480 kJ

3 leeks
1lb (500g) carrots
Mustard seeds
Crushed coriander
Sea salt
⅓oz (10g) soft vegetable margarine
1 bunch flat-leaved parsley, chopped

Trim the leeks, wash them thoroughly and cut into 2 inch (5cm) slices. Scrub the carrots, or peel if necessary, and cut them into quarters lengthways. Sweat the vegetables in a little water for 15-20 minutes with the mustard seeds and coriander. Season with salt.

Divide the vegetables in half. Add the margarine and a little parsley to the portion you are about to eat. Serve with tofu burgers.

Purée the rest of the vegetables with the remaining parsley. Stir in 2 dessertspoons fresh cream for a delicious vegetable soup (about 180 kcal 720 kJ).

Leek with Mustard Seeds

120 kcal   480 kJ

1 leek
½ cup vegetable stock
Sea salt
1 teaspoon mustard seeds
A little soft vegetable margarine

Trim the leek, wash it thoroughly and cut into slices. Sweat it in the vegetable stock with the mustard seeds for about 10 minutes, season to taste and add the margarine. This tastes good with potatoes and parsley.

Variation
Use fresh or soured cream instead of margarine, or sprinkle the cooked leek with cheese and put into a hot oven until the cheese has melted.

Sweet Carrots with Ginger

150 kcal   600 kJ

2-3 carrots
⅓oz (10g) soft vegetable
margarine
1 small onion
3-4 dessertspoons water
1 teaspoon honey
A few slices fresh ginger
Sea salt (optional)

Peel and finely slice the carrots. Heat the fat in a pan and sweat the diced onion. Add the carrots and cook for 8-10 minutes. Add the honey, fresh ginger and a little salt to taste. Serve with potato purée.

Stuffed Spinach Beet Leaves

200 kcal   800 kJ

About 7oz (200g)
spinach beet
Sea salt
1 medium onion
1 dessertspoon cracked
wheat
1 teaspoon vegetable oil
1 dessertspoon
sunflower seeds
1 dessertspoon grated
cheese (such as
Emmenthal)
1 teaspoon lemon juice
Freshly ground black
pepper
Paprika pepper

(Makes two servings)

Wash the spinach beet, blanch in salt water and drain well. Spread out the leaves and cut off the thick ribs. Chop these with the onion and brown lightly in hot fat with the cracked wheat. Allow to cool slightly, then mix with the sunflower seeds and grated cheese. Add lemon juice, pepper and paprika. Spoon this mixture onto the spinach beet leaves (you will have enough for two servings) and roll the leaves up around the filling. Tie with cotton if necessary.

Lay the rolls in an ovenproof dish and spoon over 3-4 dessertspoons fresh cream or half the quantity of basic sauce given in the recipe on page 59. Cook in the oven at 220°C (450°F, Gas Mark 8) for about 20 minutes. (Save energy by baking bread or cakes at the same time.) Serve with brown rice and salad.

Red and Green Peppers

Wash the peppers, cut them in half and take out the pith and seeds. Dice the peppers. Peel and dice the onion and sweat it in hot fat. Add the peppers and the diced tomato and cook for about 10 minutes. Sprinkle with parsley. Serve with rice.

140 kcal   560 kJ

1 red pepper
1 green pepper
1 medium onion
⅓oz (10g) soft vegetable margarine
1 beef tomato or 1 dessertspoon tomato purée
1 dessertspoon chopped parsley

Stuffed Peppers

Wash the peppers, cut them in half and take out the seeds and pith. Sweat them briefly in a little water. Prepare the filling and stuff the pepper halves with it. Sprinkle with grated cheese and bake in the oven at 220°C (450°F, Gas Mark 8) for 20-30 minutes.

Serve with potato nests, which can be cooked in the oven at the same time to save energy.

260 kcal   1040 kJ

1-2 peppers

For the filling
Follow the recipe for grain burgers (see page 113), using half for the filling and half to make three burgers
1 dessertspoon grated cheese to finish

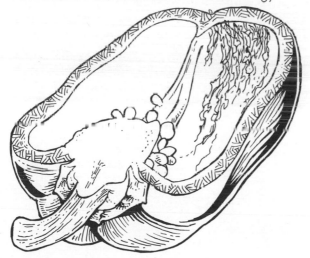

160 kcal   640 kJ

6-7oz (150-200g) field
mushrooms
1 clove garlic
2 shallots
1 dessertspoon butter
Sea salt
Freshly ground black
pepper
1 dessertspoon soya
sauce
2 dessertspoons fresh
cream
½ bunch flat-leaved
parsley

Lightning Quick Mushroom Ragoût

Trim the mushrooms, wash them and spread
them on a kitchen towel to dry. Cut up any very
large mushrooms. Peel the garlic and shallots and
chop finely. Sweat in hot butter until transparent.
Add salt, pepper, soya sauce and cream to taste.
Sprinkle with chopped parsley.

Serve these with wholemeal bread and butter,
dumplings or wholewheat spaghetti.

160 kcal   640 kJ

2 shallots
7oz (200g) fresh
chanterelles
⅓-⅔oz (10-20g) butter
and soft vegetable
margarine
Sea salt
White pepper
1 clove garlic, crushed
1 dessertspoon soured
cream
½ bunch of chervil

Chanterelles with Chervil and Garlic

Peel and slice the shallots, trim and wash the
chanterelles. Heat the butter and margarine
together and sweat the shallots gently. Add the
chanterelles, season and stir in the garlic. Add 1
or 2 dessertspoons water and cook for about 15
minutes over a low flame. Add the cream, check
the seasoning and garnish with chopped chervil.

Serve with potato purée.

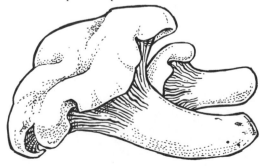

Cabbage Soufflé with Cheese

320 kcal   1280 kJ

(Makes two servings.)

Grease an ovenproof soufflé dish. Chop the cabbage finely and put half of it in the dish. Peel the potatoes, cut them in slices and layer them on top of the cabbage. Top with the remaining cabbage. Whisk the eggs together with the milk, salt, pepper and cumin and pour over the cabbage.

Cook in a preheated oven at 200°C (400°F, Gas Mark 6) for about 25 minutes. Divide the soufflé into two portions. Sprinkle one with chives and eat straight away. Sprinkle the other with cheese and return to the oven for a further 10 minutes.

Let the uneaten half cool and store in the fridge or freezer. When you are ready to eat it, sprinkle it with 1-2 dessertspoons water and a little more grated cheese and cook in the oven for 10 minutes.

Vegetable margarine to grease the dish
12oz (350g) white cabbage
8oz (250g) potatoes, cooked in their skins
2 eggs
½ cup milk
Sea salt
Freshly ground black pepper
Whole cumin seeds
1-2oz (25-50g) grated cheese
Chopped chives

Beetroot with Onions

130 kcal   520 kJ

Peel the beetroot and onion and slice thinly. Cook in the wine or vegetable stock with the lemon juice and mustard seeds for about 20 minutes. Season to taste with salt and cumin, if liked, and add the butter. Serve with potato nests.

1 beetroot
1 medium onion
½ cup dry red wine or vegetable stock
2 dessertspoons lemon juice
1 teaspoon mustard seeds
Sea salt
Ground cumin (optional)
1 teaspoon butter

200 kcal   800 kJ

1 bulb of celeriac
Sea salt
1 egg
1 dessertspoon
wholemeal breadcrumbs
or sesame seeds
Coconut fat for frying

Celeriac in Breadcrumbs

Peel the celeriac and steam it for about 40 minutes. Cut two slices, about 1.5cm thick, from the middle of the celeriac. Reserve the rest. Sprinkle the slices lightly with salt, then dip in beaten egg and in the breadcrumbs or sesame seeds. Press the crumbs or seeds on well, then fry the celeriac in hot coconut fat on both sides until golden brown. Serve with lemon wedges. Eat with other vegetable dishes.

On the following day, make a celeriac cream soup from the remaining celeriac. Purée the celeriac with 1 cup of the water that it was steamed in and 2-3 dessertspoons fresh cream. Sprinkle with fresh parsley or sprouted seeds.

130 kcal   520 kJ per portion

Asparagus stalks
Lemon juice
Butter

Asparagus with Butter

Buy good quality asparagus, firm of stalk and tightly closed at the tips. It can be kept wrapped in a damp cloth in the fridge for 2-3 days. Scrape each stalk of asparagus carefully and cut off the woody ends. Then simmer in lightly salted water with a little lemon juice for about 15 minutes, depending on size.

Save the cooking water. You can use it as a base for soups and sauces. Serve the asparagus with melted butter or a sauce of your choice.

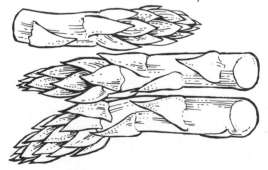

Spinach in Cheese Sauce

200 kcal 800 kJ

Wash the spinach and discard any tough stalks. Season with salt and nutmeg and cook briefly in only the water clinging to the leaves.

Chop the shallot. Heat the margarine and fry the shallot until transparent. Pour over the wine, stir in the cream and continue to cook for a few minutes. Add the cheese, stir until it melts and season with pepper. Stir the spinach into the sauce and serve with millet risotto and grilled tomatoes.

7-8oz (200-250g) fresh spinach
Sea salt
Nutmeg
⅓oz (10g) soft vegetable margarine
1 shallot
2-3 dessertspoons white wine
3-4 dessertspoons cream
2 dessertspoons grated cheese (such as Emmenthal)
Freshly ground black pepper

Spinach with Garlic

110 kcal 440 kJ

Wash the spinach and discard any tough stalks. Put it in a pan, add a little salt, cover and cook in only the water clinging to it for 2-3 minutes, until it has collapsed. Peel and chop the garlic and brown it gently in hot olive oil. Add the spinach, cook for a couple of minutes, then add the basil, pepper and lemon juice.

7-8oz (200-250g) fresh spinach
Sea salt
1-2 cloves garlic
1-2 dessertspoons olive oil
Basil
Freshly ground black pepper
1 dessertspoon lemon juice

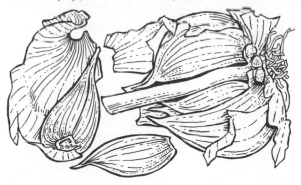

130 kcal   520 kJ

½ **savoy cabbage**
1 dessertspoon butter or
soft vegetable margarine
1 medium onion
½ **cup vegetable stock**
Sea salt
½ **teaspoon honey**
1 dessertspoon soya
sauce

Savoy Cabbage with Onion

(Makes two servings.)

Trim and wash the cabbage, discard the stalk and cut the leaves into broad strips. Peel and chop the onion and sweat it in the hot fat. Add the cabbage, pour over the stock and cook for about 10 minutes. Add salt, honey and soya sauce to taste. Eat one portion, allow the rest to cool and store it in the fridge for the next day. Add vegetable stock and eat it as soup.

Use the rest of the cabbage in a hotpot or make cabbage puffs by following the courgette recipe on page 95.

120 kcal   480 kJ

1 small savoy cabbage
1 cup vegetable stock
Sea salt
3-4 dessertspoons fresh
cream
1 dessertspoon tomato
purée
Freshly ground black
pepper

Savoy Cabbage with Tomato Cream

Wash the savoy cabbage and cut it into quarters. Cook in a very little water. Mix some of the cooking liquor with the cream and tomato purée, season with pepper and pour over the cabbage. Serve with potato purée.

Stewed Onions

	220 kcal 880 kJ

Peel and slice the onions. Sweat them gently in the butter. Pour on the stock and cook for about 10 minutes. Season with salt and coriander. Mix the cream with the egg yolk and stir into the onions. Sprinkle with parsley.

2 medium onions
1 teaspoon butter
½ cup vegetable stock
Sea salt
Ground coriander
½ carton soured cream (use the rest on muesli)
1 egg yolk (save the white for an omelette)
1 teaspoon chopped parsley

Courgettes with Soured Cream

140 kcal   560 kJ

(Makes two helpings.)

Peel and dice the onion and cook in hot fat until golden. Wash the courgettes and cut into 2cm pieces. Immerse the tomatoes briefly in boiling water, skin and chop them. Add the vegetables to the onions and cook for about 10 minutes. Add salt, pepper, basil, oregano and garlic.

Serve one portion straight away with a dollop of soured cream. Polenta makes a good accompaniment.

Add vegetable stock to the other half and make a soup out of it for the next day.

1 medium onion
1 teaspoon vegetable margarine
2-3 courgettes
2 medium tomatoes
Sea salt
Freshly ground black pepper
Fresh basil
A little dried oregano
1 clove garlic, crushed
1 dessertspoon soured cream

Vegetable Puffs

Courgette Puffs

Wash the courgettes, cut off the stalks and grate them. Pat dry with a kitchen cloth and sprinkle with lemon juice. Stir the courgettes together with the egg and cracked wheat to make a batter. Season with salt, pepper and garlic powder. Add a little more cracked wheat if the batter is too thin.

Heat some fat in a pan. Add a spoonful of batter and flatten it with the back of the spoon. Fry the puff on both sides until golden brown. Take it out of the pan and lay on absorbent kitchen paper to drain.

This recipe makes three or four puffs. They are delicious for lunch with a raw vegetable salad.

200 kcal   800 kJ

1-2 courgettes
1 teaspoon lemon juice
1 egg
1-2 dessertspoons cracked wheat
Sea salt
Freshly ground black pepper
Garlic powder
Coconut fat for frying

Carrot Puffs

Wash the carrots. Grate them and mix with the egg, wheat, salt and parsley. Fry a spoonful of the batter at a time in hot fat until golden brown on both sides.

This recipe makes four puffs, and they taste good with potato purée. They can also be eaten cold as a packed lunch.

220 kcal   880 kJ

1-2 medium carrots
1 egg
1-2 dessertspoons cracked wheat
Sea salt
1 dessertspoon chopped parsley
Coconut fat for frying

Potato Dishes

The potato has improved its image tremendously in recent years. For a long time it was branded as fattening and shunned by anyone who was figure-conscious. In fact, it is a very important and extremely nutritious food. It contains about 20 per cent starch, valuable protein, fibre, minerals and vitamins (especially vitamin C).

When you buy potatoes, make sure they are not sprouting and that they have no green patches, which indicate the presence of poisonous substances. They should be hard, firm and smooth. The ideal storage temperature for potatoes is between 4° and 8°C.

The potato is a very versatile vegetable and it is used in countless recipes, as a main dish and as an accompaniment. Cook potatoes in their skins whenever you can, as they are less nutritious if peeled first.

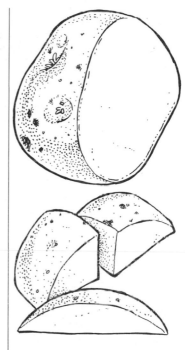

Potatoes in Foil

150 kcal   600 kJ

Scrub the potatoes and rinse them clean. Wrap them in aluminium foil and bake for about 40 minutes in the oven at 200-220°C (400°-450°F, Gas Mark 6-8), depending on their size.

Open the foil, cut a cross in the potato and season with salt, pepper and ground cumin.

You can also cut the potatoes in half and cook them on a baking tray. Here are a few ideas for serving baked potatoes;

- with butter and fresh herbs;
- with sesame butter;
- with creamed spinach (see page 91);
- with soured cream;
- with quark and herbs;
- with low-fat soft white cheese or Roquefort

2 medium potatoes
Sea salt
Freshly ground black pepper
Cumin

Creamed Potato Purée

230 kcal   920 kJ

(Makes two portions.)

About 1 lb (400-500g)
potatoes, cooked in their
skins
8 fl oz (250ml) milk
Nutmeg
Sea salt
1 dessertspoon chopped
dill
3-4 dessertspoons fresh
cream

Peel the cooked potatoes and mash them with
the milk. Season and beat or whisk until creamy.
Mix in the dill and cream.

Eat half straight away. It goes with all
vegetable dishes. With the other half you can
make one of the following three dishes.

Potato Cakes

360 kcal   1440 kJ

½ quantity of potato
purée (see above)
1-2 dessertspoons quark
1-2 dessertspoons
wholemeal flour
Seasoning and freshly
chopped herbs to taste
Coconut fat

Mix the potato purée with the quark and flour,
season to taste and form into cakes. Fry in hot
fat until golden brown on both sides. Eat with
mushrooms or a raw vegetable salad.

Creamed Potato Soup

330 kcal   1320 kJ

½ quantity of potato
purée (see above)
1 cup milk or vegetable
stock
⅓ oz (10g) soft vegetable
margarine
1 slice wholemeal bread,
cut into squares

Mix the potato purée with the milk or stock and
stir well until smooth. Put on to heat. Check the
seasoning. Heat the margarine in a pan and fry
the bread squares in it until crisp. Float the
croûtons on the soup.

Potato Nests

(Makes two portions.)

Combine the potato purée with the egg and flour.
Pipe two potato nests on a greased baking sheet
and fill them with cheese. Bake in the oven at
200°C (400°F, Gas Mark 6) for about 15 minutes.
   Serve with young carrots or stuffed aubergines,
which can be baked at the same time.

370 kcal   1480 kJ

½ quantity of potato
purée (see above)
1 egg
1 dessertspoon
wholemeal flour
1 dessertspoon grated
cheese

Potato Goulash

(Makes two portions; freeze one.)

Peel the potatoes and cut them into even-sized
cubes. Heat the fat and cook the chopped onion
in it until transparent. Add the potatoes and pour
on the stock. Cover the pan and cook for about
20 minutes. Season with salt, pepper and
paprika. Stir in the soured cream and sprinkle on
the chives. Eat with raw vegetable salad.

350 kcal   1400 kJ per
portion

About 1lb (400-500g)
potatoes
2 medium onions
8 fl oz (250ml) vegetable
stock (from a cube)
Sea salt
White pepper
Paprika pepper
1 carton soured cream
Chopped chives

Potato Puffs

Peel the potatoes, then wash and grate them.
Mix with the egg, flour and seasoning to make a
batter. Heat the fat in a pan and cook the batter
a spoonful at a time. Take the potato puffs out
when cooked and drain on absorbent kitchen
paper. Apple sauce or apple cream sauce (see
page 60) go very well with this dish.

290 kcal   1160 kJ per
portion

About 7oz (200g)
potatoes
1 egg
1 dessertspoon
wholemeal flour
Thyme
Sea salt
Freshly ground black
pepper
Coconut fat for frying

Pasta

Wholewheat pasta has a more distinctive taste than its white equivalent, it is heartier and has more 'bite'. It is, of course, more nutritious and healthier. Like all wholemeal products, it contains valuable vitamins from the B group, minerals and fibre.

If you live alone it is more practical to buy ready-made pasta in various shapes and sizes. But you will enjoy making it yourself if you can.

The dough needs a little more liquid than if you were making pasta with white flour, and you have to cook it for longer. The following recipe for wholewheat noodles will give you an idea of what is involved

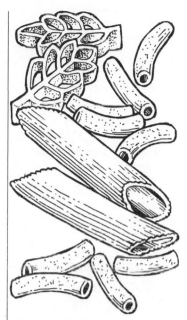

380 kcal   1520 kJ per
portion

3-4 eggs
1 teaspoon sea salt
About ¼ pint (150ml)
water
12oz (350g) finely
ground wholemeal flour

Homemade Wholemeal Noodles

(Makes four portions.)

Beat the eggs with the salt and water. Gradually stir in the flour until you have a manageable dough. Leave it to rise for about 40 minutes. Knead it thoroughly, adding a little more liquid if necessary. The dough should be smooth and elastic.

Divide the dough and roll it out piece by piece on a wooden board sprinkled with cold water. Cut the dough into strips and drop them into a pan of boiling salted water. When the noodles have risen to the surface, turn down the heat and continue to cook for about 5 minutes.

When the noodles are cooked, take them out with a slotted spoon, rinse them in hot water and drain in a sieve.

Divide the noodles into four portions. Eat one portion straight away. Toss the noodles with hot butter, garlic, herbs, tomato purée or sesame seeds, and serve with salad.

Freeze two portions. When you want to use them, drop the noodles into boiling water for just long enough to heat them up, then serve with a sauce as above.

Use the forth portion for the following recipe on the next day.

Cheesy Noodles

Heat the vegetable margarine in a pan and sweat the chopped onion until transparent. Add the noodles and cheese and continue to cook until the cheese has melted. You can also make cheesy noodles in the oven, if you are using it for baking. Serve with a salad of raw vegetables.	**400 kcal 1600 kJ** **1 portion noodles (see above)** **⅓oz (10g) soft vegetable margarine** **1 small onion** **1oz (25g) grated cheese (45 per cent fat)**

Noodle Omelette with Courgettes and Cheese

480 kcal 1920 kJ per portion

Boil the macaroni in salted water for about 10 minutes, then drain well. Fry the onion and courgette in the margarine for about 10 minutes. Add garlic, pepper and herbs to taste.

Beat the egg with the milk and stir in the cheese. Heat the fat in a pan, pour in the egg mixture, add the noodles and vegetables and cook until nearly set. Serve with a green salad.

About 2oz (50g) wholewheat macaroni
2 pints (1 litre) salted water
1 small onion, chopped
1 medium courgette, sliced
⅓oz (10g) soft vegetable margarine
1 clove garlic, crushed
Freshly ground black pepper
Dried mixed herbs
1-2 eggs
2 dessertspoons milk
2 dessertspoons grated cheese
Coconut fat for frying

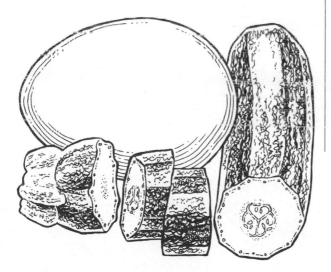

350 kcal   1400 kJ per portion

About 2oz (50g) wholewheat tagliatelle
Salted water
1 small onion
5oz (150g) fresh button mushrooms
1 bunch of parsley
⅓oz (10g) soft vegetable margarine
½ carton soured cream
Sea salt
White pepper
Cayenne pepper

Tagliatelle with Herbs and Mushrooms

Boil the tagliatelle in salted water for about 10 minutes. Drain well and keep warm.

Meanwhile, peel and chop the onions. Trim, wash and slice the mushrooms. Wash and chop the parsley. Sweat the onions in the margarine until transparent, add the mushrooms and continue to cook gently for about 10 minutes. Add the chopped parsley and cream, and season with salt, pepper and Cayenne. Mix the tagliatelle into the sauce and serve with a tomato salad.

410 kcal   1640 kJ per portion

4oz (100g) frozen spinach
Sea salt
Freshly ground black pepper
Nutmeg
2-3oz (50-80g) wholewheat spaghetti
4 pints (2 litres) water
1oz (25g) grated cheese (45 per cent fat)
2 dessertspoons soured cream (save the rest for muesli)

Wholewheat Spaghetti with Spinach

(Cut the spinach block in half with a hot knife, or an electric knife if you have one.)

Set the frozen spinach over a very low heat and cook gently for about 10 minutes. Chop roughly and season with salt, pepper and nutmeg.

Meanwhile, bring 4 pints (2 litres) water to the boil, salt it lightly and cook the spaghetti for 10-12 minutes. Drain in a colander, then return to the pan. Stir in the spinach, cheese, cream and chopped herbs. Cook over a gentle heat, stirring, until the cheese has melted. Serve with salad.

Pancakes

Have you ever tried making wholemeal pancakes? Besides being more nutritious, they are tastier and more filling than pancakes made with white flour. Pancakes make a convenient basis for a meal, because you will already have most of the ingredients in the kitchen. They are quick to make, and cheap too.

You can make pancakes with all kinds of different grain (see blinis, page 119).

The batter should be fairly thick and should always be allowed to stand for a while. If you want a very light, fluffy pancake, separate the eggs and add the whites, stiffly beaten, at the last minute. Pancakes are best fried in coconut fat.

Choose from all kinds of sweet and savoury fillings: honey, maple syrup, stewed fruit, softened dried fruit or fruit salad make a good filling for dessert or supper. Vegetable ragoût, soya sauce, cheese, mushrooms, asparagus or herbs make good savoury fillings for pancakes to be eaten as a main dish with salad.

Basic Pancake Recipe

290 kcal   1160 kJ

Whisk together the eggs, salt, milk, flour, baking powder and seasoning, using a hand or electric whisk. Let the batter stand. Heat the fat in a pan. Add a spoonful of batter and cook on both sides until golden brown.

1-2 eggs
Sea salt
3½ fl oz (100ml) milk
2-3 dessertspoons wholemeal flour
A pinch of baking powder
Nutmeg or vanilla essence, according to taste
Coconut fat for frying

480 kcal   1920 kJ

Basic pancake recipe
(see above)
5oz (150g) spinach
1 small onion
⅓oz (10g) soft vegetable
margarine
1 dessertspoon
sunflower seeds
Sea salt
Freshly ground black
pepper
Nutmeg
1 dessertspoon grated
cheese

Pancakes Filled with Spinach

Trim and wash the spinach. Chop the onion and
sweat in the fat. Add the spinach, with only the
water clinging to it, and cook gently for about 10
minutes. Add the sunflower seeds and season to
taste. Sprinkle the hot pancakes with grated
cheese, divide the spinach mixture between them,
roll them up and eat straightaway with carrot
salad.

450 kcal   1800 kJ

Basic pancake recipe
(see above)
5oz (150g) button
mushrooms
1 shallot
⅓oz (10g) soft vegetable
margarine
1 small glass white wine
Soya sauce
2 dessertspoons fresh
cream
Sea salt
1 dessertspoon sprouted
seeds (lucerne or radish
– see page 52)

Pancakes with Mushroom Filling

Trim, wash and slice the mushrooms. Dice the
shallot. Cook the shallot and mushrooms in hot
fat. Add the wine, soya sauce and cream and
continue to cook gently for about 10 minutes.
Season with salt, add the sprouted seeds and stir
well. Divide the filling between the hot pancakes
and roll them up. Serve with lamb's lettuce.

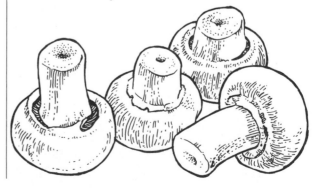

Pancakes with Fruit Filling

450 kcal   1800 kJ

Clean and slice the fruit. Cook the pancakes, dribble over the honey, add soured cream, fruit and almond slivers and roll them up.

Basic pancake recipe (see above)
1 kiwi fruit or 5oz (150g) strawberries
1 dessertspoon soured cream
1 teaspoon honey
1 teaspoon slivered almonds

Variation
Make the pancake batter and add a few finely chopped slices of apple. Sweeten with honey and sprinkle with cinnamon.

Cooking with Grain

The story of grain goes back into prehistory, long before the birth of Christ. It was one of man's first foods, and it is still a vital source of food in every part of the world.

Grain is the fruit or seed of certain grasses. The human body cannot digest raw untreated grain very easily, so for thousands of years, people have been grinding grain, soaking it, drying it, boiling it and baking it to make its vital nutrients more accessible to the human digestive juices.

Until the Middle Ages grain was eaten primarily as a sort of porridge or gruel. When the potato was introduced into Europe in the sixteenth century, it took over from grain in some of these dishes, and grain became slightly less important.

Wholegrains are a natural food reserve. Once the grain has been cracked or milled, it starts to lose its nutritive value relatively quickly, and for this reason a home mill is a worthwhile purchase even for the single-person household. You can grind as much or as little as you need each time and store small quantities in airtight dark glass jars in the fridge. You can freeze it, too.

Never keep cracked grain or wholemeal flour for any longer than four weeks before using it.

The different types of grain

The cultivation and constituents of the various types of grain are quite similar. On average, they contain about 70 per cent starch, 2-5 per cent fat, about 10 per cent protein, many vitamins (especially from the B group), minerals and, of course, fibre.

Grain can supply us with many of the vital nutrients we need, provided that we eat wholemeal, not refined products.

Wheat is the most important grain of all. There are hard and soft varieties. Durum wheat (the hard variety) has the higher protein content and is used to make pasta. Wheat is rich in gluten and is therefore ideal for baking. Dough made with wheat rises well and is firm and elastic.

You can buy wholewheat, cracked wheat, flour, flakes and special products such as bran, wheatgerm and semolina.

Rye contains gluten and is used mostly for baking bread. It is available in the form of wholegrains, cracked grains, flour, flakes and the products made from them.

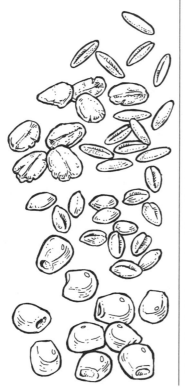

Oats contain *less* starch and *more* fat than most grains. They are useful in many dishes, though not suitable for baking. Buy wholegrains, cracked grains, flakes and grits. They are high in soluble fibre, the most valuable type of all.

Barley is the oldest known grain. It is not very good for baking, but makes excellent soups and hotpots. Available as wholegrains, pot barley (which is polished), flakes, grits and flour. From barley comes extract of malt, a natural sweetener produced by the action of enzymes.

Maize is cultivated primarily in America. Because it does not contain gluten it is difficult to bake with, but it can be made into several unusual dishes, including popcorn and sweetcorn. It is also found in the form of flakes and as semolina for making polenta.

Rice comes predominantly from Asia, where it is the staple food. It is not grown in dry fields, as other grains are, but is planted under water. Long-grain rice can be cooked so that each grain remains separate, but short-grain rice, the round pudding rice, has a more porridge-like consistency when cooked. Unpolished brown rice is the most nutritious because it has not been refined.

Parboiled rice, for example arborio, has been blanched by a steaming process which removes about 50 per cent of its minerals and vitamins as well as its brown outer skin. Though its value has been so greatly reduced, it is prized for its light colour and its quick cooking time—it needs only 20 minutes, whereas brown rice needs 40 minutes.

White rice has been refined and polished, a process that robs it of fibre, vitamins and minerals. It is also less satisfying than brown rice.

Millet was taken from Europe to Africa in the fifteenth century, and it is cultivated there today. It is quickly prepared and, with imagination, can be made into many unusual and delicious dishes. It has a particularly high silicic acid content, which is very beneficial for the connective tissues, skin, nails and hair. You can buy millet in the form of wholegrains, flour and flakes.

Buckwheat Though not classified botanically as a grain, buckwheat fits into this category as a food because of its grain-like fruit and its composition. It can grow in inclement conditions and on wasteland and heath land. It tastes quit nutty and lends itself to baking, even though it does not contain gluten. It can be bought as wholegrains, grits and flour.

If your are new to cooking with these different grains, you will be surprised how easy it is. In principle, the same methods apply to each one, but the cooking times can differ. Grain dishes keep well, and it is easy to create lots of variations on the same recipe. It is an ideal food for the small household.

Basic recipes

For a side dish you should allow about 2oz (50g) per serving; for a main dish you will need about 3oz (80g). It is a good idea to prepare more grain than you need (for one thing, you will be saving energy), then divide it into portions and freeze some to use later in another recipe. Frozen grain should be immersed very briefly in boiling water.

Wheat and spelt. Let these steep in water overnight, then cook the grain in the same water for about 50 minutes. Bring the water to the boil, then turn the heat to very low until the grains have completely swelled up. (In a pressure cooker this will take about 20 minutes.)

Rye. Soak overnight and cook in the same water for about 45 minutes.

Oats. Soak overnight and cook in the same water for 30-40 minutes.

Barley. Soak overnight and cook in the same water for about 40 minutes.

Maize. Cook for about 40 minutes.

Brown rice. Cook for about 40-45 minutes.

Millet. Rinse in hot water and cook for 20-30 minutes with the lid on.

Buckwheat. Pour boiling water over the grain and cook for about 20 minutes.

If the grains have been kiln-dried first, the cooking time will be reduced by about 10 minutes.

Grainburgers

(Makes two meals.)

Chop the onion, put the grain in the water with the salt, bay leaf and vegetable extract, bring to the boil and cook over a low heat for 15-20 minutes, or until the grains have swollen well. Let it cool, then mix in the egg, quark, breadcrumbs, pepper, onion and parsley. Season to taste, then make six flat burgers. Press them in more breadcrumbs to coat if you like. Fry in hot coconut fat on both sides until golden brown.

Eat two or three burgers with a vegetable accompaniment. The remainder can be eaten cold on the next day (you might take them to work as a packed lunch), with mustard, slices of tomato and cucumber and strips of peppers.

180 kcal   720 kJ

3oz (80g) cracked grain
7fl oz (200ml) water
Sea salt
1 bay leaf
½ teaspoon vegetable extract
1 egg
2 dessertspoons quark
1-2 dessertspoons wholemeal breadcrumbs
Freshly ground black pepper
1 small onion
2 dessertspoons chopped parsley
Coconut fat for frying

190 kcal   760 kJ

**Cooked grain, as for
grainburgers, above
2 dessertspoons
sunflower seeds
1 medium carrot
1 leek
A few mushrooms
(optional)
1 egg
1-2 dessertspoons
breadcrumbs
Freshly ground black
pepper
Sea salt
1 dessertspoon soya
sauce
Yeast extract
Coconut fat for frying**

Grain and Vegetable Burgers

Grate the carrot and slice the leek. Prepare the grain as for grainburgers. When it has cooled, mix in the vegetables, and the other ingredients, season to taste, form into burgers and fry. These burgers are less dense than grainburgers and can be eaten simply with salad.

250 kcal   1000 kJ

**About 3oz (80g) whole
rye grains
1 medium, ripe pear
1 red pepper**

For the dressing
**2oz (50g) Roquefort
cheese
1-2 dessertspoons hot
water
1 carton live yogurt (3.5
per cent fat)
Sea salt
White pepper
Flat-leaved parsley**

Rye Grain Salad with Roquefort Dressing

Soak the rye overnight and cook it in the same water for about 45 minutes (20 minutes if you are using a pressure cooker). Peel and dice the pear, wash the red pepper and take out the pith and seeds. Dice the pepper. Mash the Roquefort with hot water, then mix until smooth with the yogurt, salt and pepper. Mix all the ingredients together into the sauce. Divide into two portions. Keep one, well sealed, in the fridge. Sprinkle the other with parsley and eat straight away.

Grain Salad

Cook the grain according to the instructions given in the basic recipe on page 112, then let it cool. Dice the tomato, gherkin, onion and radishes. Chop the chives. Make the dressing with the oil, lemon juice, salt, mustard, honey and garlic and mix it in with the other ingredients. Divide into two and eat one portion for your supper with a hard-boiled egg. Save the rest to take to work (remember the garlic!).

Variation
Grain salads can be dressed with crème fraiche or any other favourite dressing.

280 kcal   1120 kJ per serving

3oz (80g) wheat, rye barley or oats
1 tomato
1 pickled gherkin
1 small onion
5 radishes
1 bunch chives

For the dressing
2 dessertspoons cold-pressed sunflower oil
Juice of half a lemon
Sea salt
1 teaspoon mustard
½ teaspoon honey
1 clove garlic, crushed

Cheesy Wheaten Bake

(Makes two servings.)

Prepare the wheat according to the basic recipe on page 112. Dice the courgette and cut the tomatoes into eight pieces. Peel and chop the onions and fry in hot fat until golden brown. Add the tomato purée, courgette and tomatoes and cook gently for a few minutes. Crush the garlic into the pan and add the basil and seasoning. Mix in the wheat and transfer the mixture to two small ovenproof dishes or one larger one. Top with slices of cheese and pour over the cream. Bake in the oven at 200°C (400°F, Gas Mark 6) for about 40 minutes. (To save energy, bake bread at the same time.)

Do not add the cheese and cream if you are going to freeze the dish. They can be added when reheating.

500 kcal   2000 kJ per serving

4-6oz (100-150g) wheat
1 dessertspoon tomato purée
1 courgette
2 medium tomatoes
2 medium onions
¾oz (20g) soft vegetable margarine
1 clove of garlic
Basil
Sea salt
Freshly ground black pepper
4oz (100g) sheep's cheese
5 dessertspoons cream

300 kcal   1200 kJ per serving

1 onion
5oz (125g) green rye, coarsely crushed
1 pint (500ml) water
Sea salt
1 bay leaf
1 onion
1 teaspoon yeast extract
1 egg
1 dessertspoon quark
1 dessertspoon chopped herbs
1 clove garlic, crushed
Sea salt
Freshly ground black pepper
Melted butter
1 dessertspoon sesame seeds

Green Rye Dumplings

(Makes two meals. Make in advance and store.)

Chop the onion coarsely. Put the green rye, bay leaf, onion, yeast extract and salt into boiling water. Bring back to the boil and cook gently for 15 minutes until the grain is well swollen (be careful — it catches easily). Let it cool.

Work in the egg, quark, herbs, garlic, salt and pepper and form between four and six dumplings with the mixture. Lower the dumplings into fiercely boiling salted water and cook them for about 15 minutes. Drain well and arrange on a serving plate. (Allow two or three dumplings to cool, then freeze them.)

Dribble melted butter over the dumplings and sprinkle them with sesame seeds. Eat with mushroom or vegetable ragoût.

300 kcal   1200 kJ per serving

½ cup whole oats
1 cup water
1 spiral of lemon peel
1 dessertspoon sultanas
A few drops vanilla flavouring
1 dessertspoon honey
1 dessertspoon coarsely chopped hazelnuts
2-3 dessertspoons fresh cream

Oats with Nuts and Honey

Put the oats in the water, bring to the boil and cook for about 40 minutes until well swollen. After 30 minutes add the lemon peel and sultanas and stir in the vanilla flavouring, honey and nuts. Pour on the fresh cream to serve and eat with fresh fruit salad or compote.

Risotto

230 kcal   920 kJ

Heat the margarine, add the onion and rice and sweat them until transparent. Pour on boiling water and add the yeast extract, salt and pepper. Bring back to the boil and cook for 40-45 minutes. Stir in the chopped parsley.

⅓oz (10g) soft vegetable margarine
1 small onion
2-2½oz (50-60g) brown rice
1 teaspoon yeast extract
Sea salt
Freshly ground black pepper
4fl oz (125ml) water
1 dessertspoon chopped parsley

Variations
Cook the risotto with garlic and curry powder or add a dessertspoon of grated cheese or tofu to serve.

Try adding finely chopped vegetables.

If there is any left over, you can eat it as salad or mix it with beaten egg and bake it in the oven.

It is a good idea to cook a larger quantity and try one of these variations for supper on the following day.

Brown Rice and Mushrooms

280 kcal   1120 kJ

Prepare the brown rice according to the instructions in the basic recipe on page 111. Chop the shallot and wash and slice the mushrooms. Heat the fat and fry the shallot and mushrooms, season to taste and add the garlic and the wine. Cook the vegetable mixture for 10-15 minutes, then mix in the rice and sprinkle with chopped parsley and cheese. Serve with a tomato sauce.

3oz (80g) brown rice
¾oz (20g) soft vegetable margarine
1 shallot
8oz (250g) mushrooms
Sea salt
Freshly ground black pepper
2-3 dessertspoons white wine
1 clove garlic, crushed
1 bunch flat-leaved parsley
1 dessertspoon grated cheese

Rice Indian Style

320 kcal   1280 kJ

3oz (80g) brown rice
1 small banana
1 small apple
1 dessertspoon sultanas
Saffron
Curry powder
Fresh ginger
1 teaspoon sunflower
seeds
1 teaspoon sesame
seeds, lightly toasted

Prepare the rice according to the basic recipe on page 111. About 10 minutes before it is cooked, slice the banana, peel and slice the apple and stir all the fruit into the rice. Season to taste with saffron, curry powder and ginger and sprinkle with sunflower and sesame seeds. Serve with a salad of home-sprouted seeds.

Polenta

(Makes two meals.)

300 kcal   1200 kJ

1 pint (500ml) water
1 teaspoon sea salt
5oz (125g) maize
semolina

Bring the water to the boil. Add the salt and semolina and cook over a low heat for about 20 minutes until thick (be careful it doesn't scorch!).

Serve half the polenta mixed with 1 dessertspoon honey and sprinkled with chopped nuts. This goes very well with softened dried fruit or cranberries.

Mix 1 teaspoon yeast extract into the rest and spread it out in a layer about 2cm thick. The next day, make the following recipe.

Baked Polenta with Cheese

280 kcal   1120 kJ

Polenta slices (see
previous recipe)
2 tomatoes
1oz (25g) grated cheese

Top the polenta slices with sliced tomato and sprinkle with grated cheese. Bake in the oven for 10-15 minutes (to save energy, bake bread or cakes at the same time). Eat with tomato purée or creamed spinach (see page 91).

Polenta also tastes very good mixed with mushrooms and herbs.

Blinis

Mix the flour with the egg, water, salt and pepper and let the batter rest for about 15 minutes. Fry it a spoonful at a time in hot coconut fat until the pancakes are golden on both sides. Blinis taste good with a quark dip and with vegetable dishes.

200 kcal 800 kJ

2 dessertspoons
buckwheat flour
1 egg
2-3 dessertspoons water
Sea salt
Freshly ground black
pepper
Coconut fat

Savoury Buckwheat Grits

Bring the milk to the boil, pour on the grits, add the salt and yeast extract and cook for about 20 minutes. Stir in the butter and herbs. This goes very well with many vegetable dishes.

280 kcal 1120 kJ

4fl oz (125ml) milk
2-2½ (50-60g)
buckwheat grits
Sea salt
1 teaspoon yeast extract
⅓oz (10g) butter
2 dessertspoons
chopped herbs

Millet Risotto

Chop the onion and dice the carrot. Rinse the millet under hot running water (otherwise it can sometimes taste slightly bitter), and fry it in the hot fat with the onion and carrot. Add salt, bay leaf and yeast extract and pour on the boiling water. Bring back to the boil, then cook over a very low heat for 20-30 minutes. This risotto goes with all vegetable dishes and with soya ragoût.

230 kcal 920 kJ

1 small onion
1 small carrot
2-2½oz (50-60g) whole
millet
10g soft vegetable
margarine
1 bay leaf
4fl oz (125ml) water
Sea salt
Yeast extract

350 kcal   1400 kJ per serving

5oz (125g) millet
6oz (150g) button mushrooms
4oz (100g) peas
⅓ (10g) butter
1 small onion
1 egg
1 carton soured cream
1 clove garlic, crushed
Sea salt
Freshly ground black pepper
Paprika pepper
Basil
1 dessertspoon grated cheese

Millet and Vegetable Bake

Cook the millet according to the instructions in the basic recipe on page 111. Trim, wash and slice the mushrooms. Peel and chop the onion. Fry the mushrooms, onion and peas in hot fat, add a very little water and sweat for 5-10 minutes. Mix the vegetables with the millet and transfer to a greased ovenproof dish. Mix the egg with the cream, garlic, seasoning and herbs, and stir into the millet. Sprinkle with grated cheese and bake at 200°C (400°F, Gas Mark 6) for about 20 minutes. Bake bread or rolls at the same time to save energy. Serve with a green salad.

Milk, Quark and Tofu

Milk and dairy products are very important in a wholefood diet. Besides protein, they contain fat, carbohydrates and many essential vitamins and minerals. Calcium is of particular interest because many people get too little of it. All this goodness is present in fresh milk straight from the cow, but so are potentially harmful bacilli, which must be neutralized before the milk can be sold for consumption. Milk is either pasteurized or submitted to ultra-heat treatment (UHT), which means that it is heated to 135°C, and cooled immediately. UHT milk keeps for far longer than pasteurized milk.

Milk, quark and the various types of fresh soft cheese (fromage frais) are very sensitive to heat and will only keep for limited periods. They should therefore be put straight in the refrigerator, especially in summer. Do not leave any of these foods on the table for too long before or after meals. 'Sell by' and 'eat by' dates will give you a guide as to the freshness of a product. These dates are only a guide, however, and many foods can be eaten after the storage period has elapsed. Always seal opened packets tightly by wrapping them in cling wrap or foil.

Recipes containing milk, buttermilk, quark and cheese have been included throughout the book, but here are a few more ideas to stimulate your imagination.

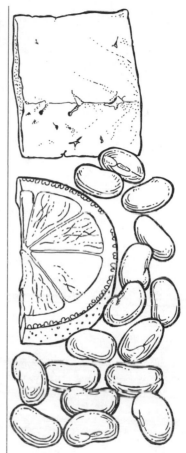

Milk Shakes and Cocktails

Make delicious drinks with milk and coffee
powder, vanilla and honey;
fruit juice concentrate;
fresh or frozen fruit;
ice cream and cocoa powder;
grated cucumber and garlic;
honey and nuts;
fruit and nut pulp;
liqueur, brandy or rum. Or use buttermilk and
add fruit juice, honey and lemon juice;
grated vegetables, pepper and herbs.

Savoury Quark

Mix quark with a variety of flavours, such as
herbs and garlic;
yeast extract;
grated vegetables;
cumin, curry powder or paprika;
cheese and herbs.

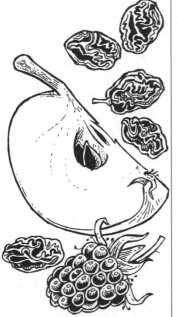

Sweet Quark

To make sweet dishes, use quark and dates and
mint;
apple and sultanas;
fruit juice concentrate;
mixed fruits and berries;
roasted nuts and honey;
maple syrup and desiccated coconut.

... and of course you can use quark and cheese
as a stuffing or mix them into oven-baked dishes.

Tofu is similar to quark and can be used in similar ways. It is a curd formed by adding a coagulate to soya milk. It is one of the staple foods in the Far East and is becoming increasingly popular in Europe. Like quark, tofu contains protein, hardly any fat, no cholesterol and very few calories. It is rich in minerals and makes a valuable addition to the wholefood diet. It is also very useful for people on slimming diets. It is very bland, but absorbs flavours well. Soft or 'siken' tofu is used in all the following recipes although a firm type is now available which can be used for stir-fry dishes and casseroles.

Tofu Dessert

180 kcal   720 kJ

(Makes two portions.)

Blend all the ingredients together in a liquidizer, sprinkle with nuts and serve one portion cold. Refrigerate the rest in the empty, washed carton (covered with clingfilm) and take to work next day for lunch.

4oz (100g) tofu
1 carton soured cream
2 dessertspoons honey or maple syrup
Lemon or orange zest
A few drops vanilla flavouring
1 dessertspoon coarsely chopped roasted nuts

Savoury Tofu

140 kcal   560 kJ

Blend all the ingredients, except for the radishes and shallots, in a liquidizer. Chop the radishes and shallots and stir into the purée. Eat this with baked potatoes in their jackets or on wholemeal bread

6oz (150g) tofu
1 teaspoon mustard
A little milk or vegetable stock
Celery salt
1 clove garlic, crushed
3-5 radishes
2 shallots

170 kcal   680 kJ

Tofu Burgers

6oz (150g) tofu
1 medium carrot
1 medium onion
1 leek (optional)
1 egg
Chopped parsley
2-3 dessertspoons
wholemeal breadcrumbs
Nutmeg
Pepper
Coconut fat for frying

(Makes two portions.)

Mash the tofu with a fork. Peel and coarsely grate the carrot, peel and chop the onion. Mix together with the egg, parsley, breadcrumbs, nutmeg and pepper. Form six small burgers from the mixture. Put them into hot fat, press them flat and fry on both sides until golden brown.

Eat some hot with vegetable dishes. Take the rest to work — they taste very good cold.

Desserts

You can make delicious desserts with milk, buttermilk, quark, fruit and cereals, and sweeten them, not with sugar, but with honey, maple syrup, concentrated pear juice and other healthy alternatives.

Fruity Quark

(Makes one large helping.)

Mix the quark and the milk together well. Stir in the fruit (whole, chopped or puréed) and add vanilla, lemon juice (optional) and honey to taste. Garnish with fruit, nuts, sunflower or sesame seeds.

240 kcal   960 kJ

5oz (125g) quark
½ cup milk (3.5 per cent fat)
About 4oz (100g) fruit, according to season
A few drops vanilla flavouring
Juice of half a lemon (optional)
1 teaspoon honey or maple syrup
1 teaspoon chopped hazelnuts
Sunflower or sesame seeds, lightly toasted

Fruit Salad with Lemon Balm

Wash and hull the strawberries. Cut them up if they are very large. Immerse the apricot briefly in boiling water, peel it and cut it into small pieces. Wash the apple well, remove the core and dice it. Mix the fruit together, squeeze over the lemon juice and add maple syrup to taste. Sprinkle with the almonds and garnish with lemon balm.

240 kcal   960 kJ

4oz (100g) strawberries
1 apricot
1 apple
Juice of half a lemon
1 teaspoon maple syrup
1 dessertspoon slivered almonds
A few leaves of lemon balm

250 kcal   1000 kJ

Peppered strawberries

8oz (250g) strawberries
Freshly ground black
pepper
1 teaspoon honey
3-4 dessertspoons fresh
cream

Wash and hull the strawberries. Cut them up if
they are very big. Sprinkle with pepper, dribble
over the honey and top with cream.

190 kcal   760 kJ

Summer Berry Dessert

5-6fl oz (150-1750ml)
buttermilk or yogurt
5oz (125g) berries
1 teaspoon pear juice
concentrate or honey
Powdered cloves
A few leaves of lemon
balm

Wash the berries thoroughly. Stir all the
ingredients together, and garnish with lemon
balm. This is a good dessert to take to work.

180 kcal   720 kJ

Baked Apple with Nuts or Sultanas

1 medium apple
1 dessertspoon quark
½ teaspoon honey
1 dessertspoon coarsely
chopped nuts or
sultanas

Wash the apple and remove the core with an
apple corer. Mix the quark with the honey and
nuts or sultanas, and spoon the mixture into the
hole in the apple.

   You can use sunflower or sesame seeds instead
of nuts. Bake in the oven at 200°C (400°F, Gas
Mark 6) for 20-30 minutes. Bake bread or pizza
at the same time to save energy.

Banana Parcel with Maple Syrup

Peel the banana, cut it in half lengthways and lay it on a square of aluminium foil. Add the wine, dribble over the maple syrup and sprinkle on the almonds. Seal the parcel and cook in the oven at 200°C (400°F, Gas Mark 6) for about 30 minutes. Bake a pizza or bread rolls at the same time to get the best out of your oven.

170 kcal   680 kJ

1 banana
1 dessertspoon white wine
1 teaspoon maple syrup
1 dessertspoon slivered almonds

Dried Fruit Salad

Soak the dried fruit overnight in 500ml water. Bring the fruit to the boil in the water it has soaked in, stir in the arrowroot and leave to cool. Add the lemon juice or white wine, vanilla and lemon balm. Sprinkle with sunflower seeds if liked. The second helping will keep well in the fridge.

150 kcal   600 kJ

2-2½oz (50-60g) dried fruit
½ teaspoon arrowroot
Lemon juice
A little white wine (optional instead of lemon juice)
A few drops of vanilla flavouring
A few leaves of lemon balm

Cracked Wheat Dessert

Bring the wheat and water to the boil, turn down the heat, cover the pan and cook slowly for about 10 minutes. Wash the berries, add them to the pan and continue to cook for a further 10 minutes. Allow the mixture to cool, sweeten with honey and serve in a wide dish with cream poured over.

200 kcal   800 kJ

1-2 dessertspoons cracked wheat
6fl oz (175ml) water
A pinch of sea salt
6oz (150g) berries of your choice
1 dessertspoon honey
5 dessertspoons single cream

250 kcal   1000 kJ

1 egg
About 6oz (150g) quark
(20 per cent fat)
1-2 dessertspoons milk
3-4 dessertspoons millet
flakes
1-2 dessertspoons honey
1 dessertspoon coarsely
chopped nuts
1 apple or 2 apricots

Quark and Millet Flakes Soufflé

Separate the egg. Mix the quark with the milk and egg yolk. Add the millet flakes, honey and nuts and the sliced apple or quartered apricot. Whip the egg white until stiff and fold it into the mixture. Pour into a greased soufflé dish and bake in the oven at 200°C (400°F, Gas Mark 6) for 30-40 minutes.

Serve with 'fruit sauce', such as apricot or peach juice. Try making this soufflé with cherries, too.

350 kcal   1400 kJ

6oz (150g) strawberries
2 scoops vanilla ice
cream
2 lemon balm leaves

Vanilla Ice with Strawberry Purée

Wash and hull the strawberries, then purée them in the blender. Put the purée on a plate, top it with the ice cream and garnish with lemon balm.

If you would like to make your own ice cream for a special occasion, follow the recipe below.

290 kcal   1160 kJ per
portion

2-3 egg yolks
1-2 dessertspoons runny
honey
A few drops vanilla
essence
7fl oz (200ml) cream (30
per cent fat)

Homemade Vanilla Ice Cream

Mix together the yolks, honey and vanilla flavouring. Whip the cream until stiff and fold it carefully into the egg. Put it into the freezer (or the ice cube compartment of the fridge) for about an hour to set. Beat it hard. Divide into four portions and freeze until solid (about 2 hours).

Home Baking for One

Wholemeal flour does not have to be coarse. On the contrary, the flour from some mills is as fine as dust. It is darker than ordinary flour, however, because the husks of the wheat are brownish in colour.

Bread and rolls are not the only things to be made from wholemeal flour. It is as versatile as ordinary flour and can be used for baking cakes and biscuits, and for making sauces, waffles, pancakes and many other dishes. Anything made with wholemeal flour has more bite, is tastier and satisfies the hunger for longer than dishes made with white flour. Here are a few tips for making and baking wholemeal dough.

- For perfect cakes and biscuits, the flour must be very finely milled. Bought wholemeal flour is often too coarse and will need to be sieved before use. Use the sieved-out bran in muesli.
- Wholemeal dough needs more liquid (about one-third more than ordinary flour), and more time to rise.
- Yeasted doughs should be allowed to rise to double their bulk.
- Always stand a tin of water in the oven when baking bread and rolls. This keeps the bread moist.
- Test to see if bread and rolls are done by tapping them underneath with your finger. If they sound hollow, they are ready.

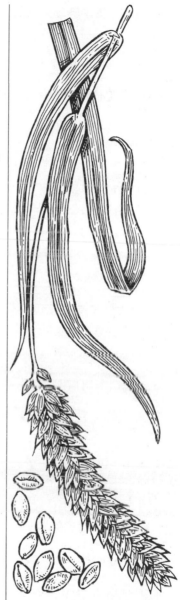

Rye Bread

120 kcal   480 kJ per 50g

12oz (350g) granary flour
10oz (300g) rye flour, sieved
10-12fl oz (300-350ml) lukewarm water
¾oz (20g) fresh yeast
1 teaspoon honey
2 teaspoons sea salt

Pour the flour into a mixing bowl and make a well in the middle. Pour a little warm water over the yeast and cream together with the honey. Add to the well in the flour. Cover the bowl with a tea towel and leave for about 15 minutes to froth up. Stir in the remaining water and salt, mix to a dough and knead well, by hand or with a mixer and a dough hook. Allow the dough to rise for about 30 minutes, then knead again. Divide the dough and form it into two rolls and two loaves. Leave them to rise for a further 30 minutes, then sprinkle with warm water and flour.

Bake in a preheated oven at 200-220°C (400-450°F, Gas Mark 6-8) for about 40 minutes. Remember to put a tin of water in the oven to keep the bread moist.

The two bread rolls will serve as one meal, perhaps to take to work. Use one of the loaves immediately, keeping it in a stone bread jar, and freeze the other.

Sesame Bread

130 kcal   520 kJ

1lb 5oz (600g) wholemeal flour (use half granary, half finely ground)
About ½ pint (300ml) buttermilk
1½oz (40g) dried yeast
1 teaspoon honey
1-2 teaspoons sea salt
3 dessertspoons sesame seeds

Pour the flour into a bowl and stir in the buttermilk (which should be lukewarm), yeast, honey, salt and about half of the sesame seeds. Let the dough rise for about 40 minutes. Knead and form into three small loaves. Let it rise again. Sprinkle with the remaining sesame seeds, brush with water (using a pastry brush) and bake in a preheated oven at 200-220°C (400-450°F, Gas Mark 6-8) for about 40 minutes.

Eat one loaf straight away — it will keep for about a week. Freeze the other loaves.

Wholemeal Rolls

(These freeze well. See page 114 for suggestions about using the remaining wholegrains.)

Prepare the grain according to the basic recipe on page 112, then mix it with all the other ingredients to make a dough. Knead the dough well and let it rise for about 30 minutes. Divide the dough and form eight rolls. Let them rise for a further 20 minutes.

Brush the rolls with warm water and bake in a preheated oven at 200°C (400°F, Gas Mark 6) for about 25 minutes.

Wholemeal bread rolls will keep for much longer than white rolls, but if you have some that are several days old and need freshening up, here's what to do. Cut them in half, fill them with a mixture of grated cheese, chopped herbs and crushed garlic, sprinkle them with water and bake in the oven until hot through. They will taste as fresh as if they had been newly baked.

200 kcal 800 kJ per roll

**2-3 dessertspoons
wholegrains of your
choice
7oz (200g) finely ground
wholemeal flour
¾oz (20g) dried yeast
(though fresh yeast
keeps for two weeks in
the fridge)
3½-5fl oz (100-150ml)
warm milk
2 dessertspoons cold-
pressed vegetable oil
Powdered onion or garlic
Sea salt
Freshly ground black
pepper**

Quark Rolls

125 kcal   500kJ per roll

(Makes 8-10 rolls. They will keep for 2-3 days. Freeze the ones you are not going to eat straight away.)

8oz (250g) finely ground
wholemeal flour
1 teaspoon baking
powder
½ teaspoon sea salt
Fennel seeds
Crushed anis
1-2 dessertspoons honey
6oz (150g) quark
A little milk if necessary
1 egg

Mix the flour, baking powder, salt and spices well together. Work in the honey, quark and egg by hand, adding a little milk if necessary to make a smooth dough. Let the dough rise. Form it into oval rolls and place them on a greased baking sheet. Brush the rolls with luke warm milk and bake in a preheated oven at 200°C (400°F, Gas Mark 6) for 20-25 minutes.

Currant Buns

165 kcal   660 kJ per roll

(Makes about 8 rolls; good for freezing.)

8oz (250g) finely ground
wholemeal flour
¾oz (20g) dried yeast
4fl oz (125ml) milk
2oz (50g) butter
2 dessertspoons honey
Cinnamon
Cardamom
Sea salt
3 dessertspoons currants

Pour the flour into a bowl, add the yeast and stir in the lukewarm milk and melted butter. Add the honey and spices. Roll the currants in flour and add to the mixture. Knead the dough well. Let it rest for 30 minutes, then knead again and form into eight buns. Let them rise again, then bake in a preheated oven at 200°C (400°F, Gas Mark 6) for about 25 minutes.

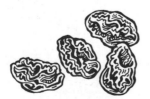

Pizza

(Makes one meal; freeze the rest of the dough.)

Mix all the ingredients together and knead well. The dough should be soft but not sticky. Roll out a quarter of the dough for the pizza base. Divide the rest into three portions and freeze it. This dough can be used for savoury cakes, mixed with leeks, onions and tomatoes, and for sweet cakes, mixed with chopped apples, plums, apricots and nuts.

Mix the tomato paste with the olive oil, garlic and seasoning. Spread this mixture on the pizza base.

Slice the tomatoes, mushrooms and onion finely and arrange them neatly on top of the pizza. Season again and sprinkle with cheese. Top with the olives.

Bake in a preheated oven at 200°C (400°F, Gas Mark 6) for about 20 minutes.

Variations
Other pizza toppings can be made with leeks, onions and spinach. Instead of the cheese, beat an egg with a little cream and spread it on top.

For the dough
6oz (150g) quark
3 dessertspoons milk
5 dessertspoons cold-pressed sunflower oil
1 egg
¾oz (20g) baking powder
1 teaspoon sea salt
12oz (350g) wholemeal flour, finely ground

For the topping
2 dessertspoons tomato paste
1 teaspoon olive oil
1 clove garlic, crushed
Mixed dried herbs
Sea salt
2 tomatoes
1 small onion
5-6 mushrooms (optional)
1oz (25g) grated cheese
A few olives

Carrot Tart and Nut Cake

(One basic mixture is used to make two different cakes. Each cake divides into six or eight pieces.)

250 kcal   1000 kJ per piece

4-5 eggs
6oz (150g) honey
1 pinch each cloves and cinnamon
2 dessertspoons kirsch

For the carrot tart
6oz (150g) carrots, finely grated
4oz (100g) ground nuts
2 dessertspoons wholemeal flour, sieved
A little grated lemon peel
A pinch of baking powder

For the nut cake
6oz (150g) ground nuts
2 dessertspoons quark
1 teaspoon cocoa
2-3 dessertspoons wholemeal flour, sieved
A pinch of baking powder

Separate the eggs. Put the whites to one side. Cream the yolks with the honey and spices. Divide the mixture into two.

Mix the carrot tart ingredients well with half the yolk mixture, and the nut cake ingredients with the other half. Whip the egg whites until they form stiff peaks. Fold half into each mixture. Transfer the carrot mix to a springform pan 6-7 inches (15-18cm) in diameter, and the nut mix to a small loaf tin, or bun tins if preferred.
   Bake them both in a preheated oven at 200°C (400°F, Gas Mark 6) for about 40 minutes.

Basic Recipe for Wholemeal Sponge Roll or Sandwich Cake

260 kcal   1040 kJ per slice (with filling)

4 eggs
2-3 dessertspoons honey
3 dessertspoons cold water
7oz (200g) finely ground wholemeal flour
2oz (50g) ground nuts
½ teaspoon baking powder

Separate the eggs, being careful that none of the yolk gets into the white. Cream together the yolks, honey and water. Stir in the flour, nuts and baking powder, mixing well. Whip the egg whites until stiff and fold into the biscuit mix. Mix well.

Line a swiss roll tin with greased greaseproof paper. Spread the mixture onto this and bake in a preheated oven at 180°C (350°F, Gas Mark 4) for about 20 minutes. Release the greaseproof paper and roll the sponge up in a damp tea towel. Alternatively, leave it flat, cut it into two and make a sandwich cake. Either will serve six or eight people. If you are not entertaining, you can freeze three quarters of the cooked cake mixture to fill and eat later.

Raspberry cream filling
(to fill one quarter of the cake)
3fl oz (100ml) cream
5oz (125g) raspberries
1 teaspoon honey
A few drops vanilla flavouring

Whip the cream until stiff and mix in the raspberries, honey and vanilla flavouring. Spread the mixture on the cake base and top with another slice of cake.

Banana cream filling
(to fill one quarter of the cake)
1 small banana
3fl oz (100ml) cream
1 teaspoon honey or maple syrup
½ teaspoon lemon juice

Mash the banana, prepare the filling and fill the cake as above.

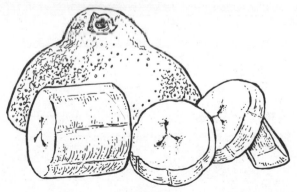

Fruit Tartlets

(Makes six or eight tartlets. They freeze well.)

240 kcal   960 kJ per tartlet

Combine the flour with the baking powder, make a well in the middle and put in the egg, salt and honey. Cut the butter into tiny pieces and dot them round the edge. Work all the ingredients to a smooth dough (let it stand a while if it starts to get sticky).

For the pastry
8oz (250g) finely ground wholemeal flour
1 teaspoon baking powder
1 egg plus 1 yolk
A pinch of salt
5-6 dessertspoons honey
4oz (100g) cold butter

Roll the dough out and line 6-8 tartlet tins with it. Bake blind for about 20 minutes in a preheated oven at 200°C (400°F, Gas Mark 6). Let the pastry cool.

Wash and trim the fruit, slice and arrange neatly in the tartlet cases. Mix the fruit juice with the agar agar according to the instructions on the packet and pour carefully over the fruit. Sprinkle on the slivered almonds.

For the filling
Mixed fruit
1 cup strawberry or other fruit juice
½ teaspoon agar agar or other vegetable gelling agent
2 dessertspoons slivered almonds

Instead of the agar agar glaze, you can simply add whipped cream.

Hazelnut Biscuits

(Makes about 30 biscuits. Store in an airtight tin.)

65 kcal   260 kJ each

Mix the flour with the baking powder and make a well in the middle. Cut the butter into small pieces, add the remaining ingredients and mix well to a smooth dough. Let it stand for about an hour. Divide the dough to roll it out. Cut the biscuits with a biscuit cutter. Brush the tops of the biscuits with milk, then decorate them with the whole nuts.

8oz (250g) finely ground wholemeal flour
1 teaspoon baking powder
4 dessertspoons honey
1 egg
A few drops vanilla flavouring
4oz (100g) soft vegetable margarine
8oz (250g) ground hazelnuts
A little milk (optional)
About 30 hazelnuts to decorate

Bake in a preheated oven at 200°C (400°F, Gas Mark 6) for 10-15 minutes.

Quick Teatime Biscuits

(Makes about 25 biscuits. They keep well for several days.)

Cream the eggs with the honey. Add the remaining ingredients and mix well. Spoon the mixture into small mounds on a baking sheet lined with greased greaseproof paper, and bake in a preheated oven at 190-200°C (375-400°F, Gas Mark 5-6) for 10-15 minutes.

45 kcal   180 kJ per biscuit

3 eggs
2 dessertspoons honey
Grated orange rind
4-5oz (100-125g) wholemeal flour
A few drops vanilla flavouring
½ level teaspoon baking powder

Cheese Straws

(Makes 30-35 cheese straws. Serve with wine.)

Work the flour, eggs, cheese and butter to a dough and let it rest in the fridge for about 30 minutes. Roll it out and cut it into strips 2-5cm wide. Brush the straws with egg yolk and sprinkle on the poppy seeds or decoration of your choice.
  Bake in a preheated oven at 200°C (400°F, Gas Mark 6) for about 10 minutes.

60 kcal   240 kJ per straw

7oz (200g) finely ground wholemeal flour
2 eggs
About (150g) grated cheese (such as Emmenthal, 45 per cent fat)
3-3½oz (80-90g) butter
1 egg yolk
Poppy seeds, cumin seeds, sesame seeds or grated cheese to decorate

Storing baked goods

Bear the following points in mind when storing bread and rolls:

1. Though cakes can always be stored in the fridge, the same is not true of bread and rolls, except in very sultry weather.

2. The best place to store bread is in an old-fashioned stone bread crock. If you do not have one of these, a bread bin will do or, failing that, keep your bread in the oven.

3. Moister types of bread keep fresh for longer.

4. Mould forms easily in moist warm conditions where air does not circulate. Check bought packaged loaves after a few days.

Fasting at the Weekend

A bewildering number of 'cures' are on offer nowadays. So much so that you could be forgiven for suspecting some institutions of cashing in on a novelty rather than taking a serious interest in their treatment or its results.

Fasting (going completely without food) and part-fasting (where only a few foods are taken in limited quantities) do not come into this category. They have both been practised for centuries and are an important part of almost all religions, because of the belief that fasting purifies the body and the spirit.

In today's high pressure world, fasting is more valid than ever. You can fast safely for a weekend, following the guidelines below. A longer fast should be undertaken only after consultation with your doctor. After a weekend's fasting you will feel very light and wonderfully well, and you will have recharged your energy for the coming week.

You should drink a lot (at least 4 pints/2 litres a day of herbal tea or still mineral water), avoid fats, sugar and salt and take gentle exercise in the fresh air.

Fasting enables the body to function properly again. It restores the balance between acids and alkalis, eliminates all waste products from the kidneys and intestines, and breaks down excess stores of fat.

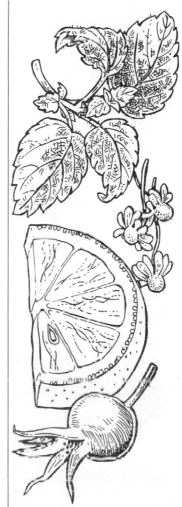

Tea-Only Fast

Method. Drink about 4-6 pints (2-3 litres) herbal tea a day. You can add a little lemon juice, but do not take too much because of the acid content. Do not drink only fruit teas for the same reason.

Details. Contains no calories.

Effects. As described above.

Bircher-Benner's Raw Vegetable Fast

Method. For this partial fast you are allowed fruit and vegetable juices, raw vegetable salads, small quantities of dried fruit, grain, honey and cold-pressed vegetable oils.

Details. Calorie content depends very much on the amounts of oil and grain consumed. High in vegetable fat and protein, vitamins, minerals, fibre, potassium. Low in sodium.

Effects. Improvement in the function of the metabolism and the circulation. Increases elimination of water, waste products and sodium. Has a beneficial influence on inflammations and allergies. Stimulates the digestion. Regulates a high blood-pressure and improves the body's natural defences.

Rice Fast

Method. Cook 8-10oz (250-300g) brown rice (dried weight) without fat or salt, divide into four or five portions and eat through the day. Serve the rice with fruit, steamed vegetables or herbs, but do not season with salt or use any other seasoning containing sodium.

Details. Low in fat and sodium, high in potassium. Very satisfying.

Effects. Encourages the elimination of water and sodium, stimulates the circulation and regulates high blood-pressure. Very beneficial for pregnant women.

Index